KAY ARTHUR

HARVEST HOUSE PUBLISHERS
Eugene, Oregon 97402

Except where otherwise indicated, all Scripture quotations in this book are taken from the New American Standard Bible, © 1960, 1962, 1963, 1968, 1971, 1972, 1973, 1975, 1977 by The Lockman Foundation. Used by permission.

Verses marked KJV are taken from the King James Version of the Bible.

Except where otherwise indicated, all maps and charts in this book, as well as the *"How to Use the Inductive Study Approach"* portion of the introductory material, have been adapted and condensed from the *International Inductive Study Bible*, Copyright © 1992, 1993 by Precept Ministries.

Cover illustration and interior art by Micha'el Washer

The International Inductive Study Series
GOD'S ANSWERS FOR RELATIONSHIPS AND PASSIONS

Published by Harvest House Publishers
Eugene, Oregon 97402

Library of Congress Cataloging-in-Publication Data

Arthur, Kay, 1933–
God's answers for relationships and passions / Kay Arthur.
p. cm. — (International inductive study series)
ISBN 1-56507-303-7
1. Bible. N.T. Corinthians—Study and teaching
2. Bible. N.T. Corinthians—Criticism, interpretation, etc. I. Title.
II. Series: Arthur, Kay, 1933– International inductive study series.
BS2675.5.A72 1995 94-47483
227'.2'007—dc20 CIP

Printed in the United States of America.

95 96 97 98 99 00 — 10 9 8 7 6 5 4 3 2 1

CONTENTS

How to Get Started . . .

It may be tempting to skip this part of the book and rush to the beginning of your study, but don't! I can relate! But in this case, this short section contains invaluable help for understanding what you will do in the study. These instructions are an integral part of getting started, and they will help you greatly!

FIRST

Let's talk about what you are going to need in order to do this study. In addition to this book, you will need four "tools":

1. A Bible (I recommend using an *International Inductive Study Bible* [IISB]. It's ideal for this kind of study because of its easy-to-read type, wide margins, single-column text, high-quality paper, and innumerable study helps.)
2. A set of colored pencils or an eight-color Pentel pencil (available at most office supply stores)
3. A composition book or notebook for working on your assignments and recording your insights
4. A four-color ballpoint pen for marking your Bible

SECOND

Though you will be given specific instructions for each day's study, there are basic things you'll want to look for and do as you study each book chapter by chapter. Let me list them for you. Read through the list but don't be overwhelmed. Eventually, each step will become a habit.

1. As you read each chapter, train yourself to ask the "5 W's and an H": who, what, when, where, why, and how. Asking questions like these helps you see exactly what the Word of God is saying. When you interrogate the text with the 5 W's and an H, ask questions like this:

a. **What** is the chapter about?
b. **Who** are the main characters?
c. **When** does this event or teaching take place?
d. **Where** does this happen?
e. **Why** is this being done or said?
f. **How** did it happen?

2. There are certain key words that you will want to mark in a special way in the text of your Bible. This is the purpose of the colored pencils and the colored pen. Developing the habit of marking your Bible in this way will make a significant difference in the way you study and in how much you remember.

A **key word** is an important word that is used by the author repeatedly in order to convey his message to his reader. Certain key words will show up throughout the book as a whole, while other key words will be concentrated in certain chapters or segments of the book. You will want to mark key words and their pronouns (*he, his, she, her, it, we, they, us, our, you, them, their*) as well as any synonyms in a distinguishable color or way.

For instance, one of the key words in 1 Corinthians is *gospel*. I put a hot-pink megaphone around the word

gospel and then color it in with green. I use the megaphone because God tells us we are to proclaim the gospel.

You need to devise a color-coding system for key words so that when you look at a page of your Bible, you will instantly see where a particular word is used. When you start marking key words in various colors and symbols, it is easy to forget how you are marking certain words. Therefore, you will find it helpful to take a three-by-five or five-by-seven card, cut it in half lengthwise, write the key words you are marking throughout the book on the card, color code them, and then use the card as a bookmark as you work through the book you are studying.

In 1 Corinthians you will use your bookmark to track certain words that are key to the book. Additionally, I will give you other key words that are used only in specific passages. In 2 Corinthians the key words are more specific to chapters or passages than they are relevant to the entire book, so I will give you the key words as you go through the study.

I mark the word *power* the same way throughout my *International Inductive Study Bible*. I color it red and draw a stick of dynamite around it: **power**. And references to the devil and his cohorts stand out because I mark these with a red pitchfork **Satan**. I color the word *wisdom* pink and then underline it in blue. When I mark *boast*, I also color it pink, but I box it with green.

Marking words for easy identification can be done using colors, symbols, or a combination of colors and symbols. However, colors are easier to distinguish than symbols. If I use symbols, I keep them very simple. For example, I color *repent* yellow and put a red arrow over it: **repent**. The symbol conveys the meaning of repent: a change of mind.

When I mark the members of the Godhead (which I do not always mark), I color every reference to the Father, Son, and Holy Spirit in yellow. I also use a purple pen and mark the Father with a triangle **God**, symbolizing the Trinity. I mark the Son this way **Jesus**, and the Holy Spirit like this: **Spirit**.

3. Because locations are important in a historical or biographical book of the Bible, you will also find it helpful to mark these in a distinguishable way. I simply underline every reference to location in green (grass and trees are green!), using my four-color ballpoint pen.

I also look up the locations on maps so I can put myself into context geographically. If you have an *International Inductive Study Bible* you will find the pertinent maps placed right in the text you are studying for ready reference.

Although locations are not essential to your understanding of 1 Corinthians, you will find that marking them in 2 Corinthians will be helpful.

4. When you finish studying a chapter, record the main theme of that chapter on the AT A GLANCE chart provided for you under the appropriate chapter number. (If you have an *International Inductive Study Bible*, you will want to record the chapter themes on the AT A GLANCE chart at the end of each book in your Bible. Then you will have a permanent record of your studies right at your fingertips.)

5. If you are doing this study within the framework of a class and you find the lessons too heavy, then simply do what you can. To do a little is better than to do

nothing. Don't be an "all or nothing" person when it comes to Bible study.

Remember, any time you get into the Word of God, you enter into more intensive warfare with the enemy. Why? Every piece of the Christian's armor is related to the Word of God. And our one and only offensive weapon is the sword of the Spirit, which is the Word of God. The enemy wants you to have a dull sword. Don't cooperate! You don't have to!

6. Always begin your studies with prayer. As you do your part to handle the Word of God accurately, you must remember that the Bible is a divinely inspired book. The words that you are reading are truth, given to you by God that you might know Him and His ways. These truths are divinely revealed. "For to us God revealed them through the Spirit; for the Spirit searches all things, even the depths of God. For who among men knows the thoughts of a man except the spirit of the man, which is in him? Even so the thoughts of God no one knows except the Spirit of God" (1 Corinthians 2:10,11).

Therefore, ask God to reveal His truth to you, to lead you and guide you into all truth. He will, if you will ask.

THIRD

This study is designed to put you into the Word of God on a *daily* basis. Since man does not live by bread alone but by every word that comes out of the mouth of God, we each need a daily helping.

The weekly assignments cover all seven days; how ever, the seventh day is different from the other days. On the seventh day, the focus is on a major truth covered in that week's study.

You will find a verse or two to memorize and STORE IN YOUR HEART. Then there is a passage to READ AND DISCUSS. This will be extremely profitable for those who are using this material in a class setting, for it will cause the class to focus their attention on a critical portion of Scripture. To aid the individual and/or the class, there's a set of OPTIONAL QUESTIONS FOR DISCUSSION. This is followed with a THOUGHT FOR THE WEEK which will help you understand how to walk in the light of what you learned.

When you discuss the week's lesson, be sure to support your answers and insights from the Bible itself. Then you will be handling the Word of God in a way that will find His approval. Always examine your insights by carefully observing the text to see *what it says*. Then, before you decide *what a Scripture or passage means*, make sure you interpret it in the light of its context.

Scripture will never contradict Scripture. If it ever seems to, you can be certain that somewhere something is being taken out of context. If you come to a passage that is difficult to deal with, reserve your interpretations for a time when you can study the passage in greater depth.

Books in *The International Inductive Study Series* are survey courses. If you want to do a more in-depth study of a particular book of the Bible, we would suggest you do a Precept Upon Precept Bible Study Course on that book. You may obtain more information on these studies by contacting Precept Ministries, P.O. Box 182218, Chattanooga, TN 37422, 615/892-6814, or by filling out and mailing the response card in this book.

First Corinthians

Relationships and Passions Transformed . . .

When you take an honest, unprejudiced, realistic look around you, you see that man doesn't have a lasting, working solution to his personal relationships and passions. Relationships are broken—shattered into a thousand jagged edges. Passions are uncontrolled and destructive.

Are there answers? Is there a solution? Or have we gone too far? Is our course so set that there is no turning away?

If it depended on man, the answer would be "Yes"—no turning around, no turning back.

But there is God! And because He is God there are answers. They may not be answers you like or want, but if you are looking for a solution that works—one that will last and carry you through the most difficult of situations—then God's answers are what you need. And you will find many of them in the books of 1 and 2 Corinthians.

You are going to be awed at what an incredibly practical study this is going to be . . . awed and, hopefully, transformed. The transformation will depend on what you do with what you learn. Go for it, my friend, and you'll find God's answers to personal relationships and passions.

Week One

God Chooses "Nobodys" and Makes Them "Somebodys"

Day One

Read 1 Corinthians 1 today. As you read, mark every reference to the recipients of this letter in a specific color so you can see what the author says about them. Be certain to mark all synonyms and pronouns referring to the recipients.

Then, in your notebook, make a chart with two headings: DESCRIPTION OF THE RECIPIENTS and PAUL'S CONCERNS FOR THE CORINTHIANS. List first how the recipients are described, then note Paul's concerns in regard to them. Note, too, what form the quarrels take and whom they center around. Keep this in mind as you continue this study.

On your 1 CORINTHIANS AT A GLANCE chart (page 72) fill in any other information you observe from chapter 1.

Day Two

Whenever you study a book of the Bible, it is always good to read the book through several times in order to discern the author's purpose for writing the book. This also enables you to see the way he lays out his material in order to achieve his purpose.

By the way, if you did not read the instructions at the beginning of this book, now is the time to stop and do so. They provide clear instructions on how to mark key words.

After reading the introduction section you know how to make a bookmark for your key words. On your bookmark for 1 Corinthians write the following key words and color code each word as you will color code it in your Bible. Remember, I gave you examples of how I mark some of my key words!

divisions[1]
gospel
power[2]
wisdom (wise, wiser)[3]
boast (boasts, boasting)[4]

These are the words you will want to mark throughout the entire book. They are not all of the key words you will mark in 1 Corinthians. As you work through this study I will give you others which are specific to certain chapters or passages.

Since this is a survey course and there isn't time for repeated readings of the book, look at 1 Corinthians 1:10,11 to see the first of Paul's purposes in writing this first epistle to the church at Corinth. Record this purpose on your 1 CORINTHIANS AT A GLANCE chart.

There is a key repeated phrase used in 1 Corinthians 7:1,25; 8:1; 12:1; 16:1 which will reveal Paul's second reason for writing to the Corinthian church. Look at these Scriptures and mark each use of the phrase *now concerning.*[5] Include in your marking whatever topic the author is about to address, if he states it. For example, you would mark the following phrases the same way you marked the phrase *now concerning*: "Now concerning the things about which you wrote"[6] and "Now concerning things sacrificed to idols,"[7] etc.

You will discover that these people had questions about certain topics and Paul was writing to answer those questions after he dealt with the problem stated in 1 Corinthians 1:10,11. Thus, you have the book of 1 Corinthians falling into two major segment divisions. Look at the chart, 1 CORINTHIANS AT A GLANCE, on page 72 and notice the section called Segment Divisions. This indicates the major break of the book into two topics. Fill in the division sections, in light of what you see.

DAY THREE

Read 1 Corinthians 1 again. This time mark key words from your bookmark.

When you finish, look at the word *wisdom* and its synonyms. What two kinds of wisdom are referred to in this chapter? Write them in your notebook as separate headings.Then, under each heading, list what you learn about these two kinds of wisdom. You will add more to this list later, so leave adequate space for more information.

DAY FOUR

Read 1 Corinthians 2 today. Mark the same key words along with the references to the recipients that you marked in 1 Corinthians 1. Add *Spirit*[8] to your bookmark and mark every reference to the Spirit. Of course, adding the word to your bookmark means you will look for it throughout the remainder of the book.

DAY FIVE

Read through the first two chapters of 1 Corinthians again. This time, in a different color, mark references to the author. While you may not want to color every "our" or every single pronoun, you should color every major reference to the author that gives you insight into who he is, what he does or has done, and what his relationship to the Christians in Corinth is.

Then set aside several pages in your notebook for a list of what you learn about the author. You will add to this throughout your study. You may want to add what you will learn in 2 Corinthians to this list too, so consider that in leaving space. Record on your list all you learn in these first two chapters of 1 Corinthians. Compiling this list may seem tedious, but you will be pleasantly surprised and enlightened by all that you learn from Paul's example.

When you finish your list, stop and think through all you have recorded. What you learn will help you follow his injunction in 1 Corinthians 4:16 and 11:1 where he says you are to be an imitator or follower of him, even as he is of Christ.

DAY SIX

Today, read through 1 Corinthians 1 and 2 again,

paying careful attention to the flow of thought. What is the main theme of each of these chapters? If you had to tell someone what these two chapters are about, what would you say? Write down your thoughts on a piece of paper, then reduce the theme to as few words as possible (try to use words from the chapter itself). Record these themes on the appropriate line of the 1 CORINTHIANS AT A GLANCE chart on page 72.

List in your notebook anything new you learn about the Corinthians from 1 Corinthians 2. Then add to your list on wisdom what you learn from 1 Corinthians 2.

Finally look at every reference to power in chapters 1 and 2. Examine these references in the light of the 5 W's and an H: who, what, when, where, why, and how. You may not find an answer to each W and H, but asking these questions will help you see what these chapters tell you about power.

DAY SEVEN

Store in your heart: 1 Corinthians 1:30,31 or, if you are up to it, memorize 1 Corinthians 1:21-24.

Read and discuss: 1 Corinthians 1:17–2:16.

OPTIONAL QUESTIONS FOR DISCUSSION

- Who wrote the book of 1 Corinthians and to whom?
- Why was 1 Corinthians written? Support your answer with Scripture.

- What did you learn about the author in the first two chapters? About the recipients? Discuss what you recorded in your notebook.
- What did you learn about wisdom and the wise from your study this week?
- How does what you learned compare with what we are to boast about? Or, to put it another way, Where is our boasting to be and why? What does this tell you about our capabilities?
- What do you learn about the Spirit of God from 1 Corinthians 2?
- How does a Christian have the mind of Christ?
- Where is power found and how does one tap into this power?
- What was the most significant insight you received this week? How will it impact your daily life?

THOUGHT FOR THE WEEK

O my friend, was it clear to you that God is looking for "nobodys" so that He can make "somebodys" out of them?

Did you see that truth with your own eyes? Did you fully comprehend what God said in 1 Corinthians 1:26-31? Or have you looked at yourself and always thought that you could never be very much for God or for His kingdom because of where you've been, what you've done, or simply because of what you are—or what you've been told you are?

It is time, Beloved, to believe God—to understand that what you are is not what God needs. God is YHWH: Yahweh, Jehovah, the all-sufficient God who is "I AM." "I AM" everything and anything you will ever need. God needs nothing. He has it all. He is all and all.

If you are *in* Christ Jesus, you have everything you need because you have God. Jesus became to you wisdom, righteousness, sanctification, and redemption. You've been redeemed—you are His and He is yours! And this, my friend, is your only place of boasting.

So boast in Him and go forward in faith's confidence and God's power. Remember, you are a "somebody" chosen by God.

Week Two

Could the Problem be "Carnality"— Are You and Others Acting Like Mere Men?

Day One

Read 1 Corinthians 3 today and mark every reference to the recipients as you did in chapters 1 and 2. If you read this chapter aloud each time you study it, it will help you remember its content. When you repeat something aloud over and over, eventually you will have it memorized. There's nothing more profitable than memorizing Scripture!

Day Two

Add *temple* to your list of key words on your bookmark. Then read 1 Corinthians 3 again and mark all the key words. By the way, the Greek* word for temple in this chapter is *naos*. The word *naos* refers to the temple

---

*From time to time we will look at the definition of a word in the Greek. Since the New Testament was originally written in Koine Greek, sometimes it is helpful to go back to the Greek to see the original meaning of a word. There are many study tools to help you if you would like to do this type of digging. One excellent book to help you understand how to do more in-depth study is *How to Study Your Bible* (Harvest House Publishers, 1994).

itself or to the inner sanctuary, the Holy of Holies, the heart and center of the whole sacred enclosure called the temple of God (*hieron*). Think about it and note what God says about the temple The word *naos* is also used in 1 Corinthians 6:19.

When you finish, record your insights on the recipients in your notebook as you did last week. Carefully note how Paul describes them. Watch the terms he uses.

Day Three

Read 1 Corinthians 3 again. This time mark every reference to the author, Paul. Also mark the pronoun *us* when it includes Paul. When you finish, add to your author information list all you learn from marking these references. Also note what you learn about Apollos from this chapter.

Day Four

Read 1 Corinthians 3 one more time. This time, watch Paul's mixed metaphors in this chapter: field,[9] planted and watered, then foundation, building and the materials that can be used to build upon the foundation. (A metaphor is an implied comparison between two things that are different.)

Think about who does the building, what they can build with, what they are held accountable for, and the consequences of it all.

DAY FIVE

Read through 1 Corinthians 4 and mark every reference to the author. Watch the flow of thought from chapter 3 to chapter 4.

DAY SIX

Read 1 Corinthians 4 again and mark every reference to the recipients, along with any other key words from your bookmark.

In your notebook list what you learn about the recipients. Then analyze the problem that Paul is dealing with in this chapter and why he says he is writing what he is. What reason would Paul possibly have to come to them with a rod? Does he have a right to do that? Why?

Record the themes of chapters 3 and 4 on the 1 CORINTHIANS AT A GLANCE chart on page 72.

DAY SEVEN

Store in your heart: 1 Corinthians 3:1-3 or 3:12,13.
Read and discuss: 1 Corinthians 1:10-13; 3:1-23.

OPTIONAL QUESTIONS FOR DISCUSSION

- How would you describe the situation Paul is addressing in 1 Corinthians 3? What's the problem and why? How does it relate to what Paul says in 1 Corinthians 1:10-13?

- What did you learn about the Corinthians from 1 Corinthians 3?
- How would you describe "fleshly" (carnal or worldly) just from this chapter, since, in 1 Corinthians, the term is used only in this chapter, and remain true to the text? (By "remain true to the text" I mean letting the text say what it says without adding to it.)
- What did you learn from 1 Corinthians 3 and 4 about Paul's relationship to the church at Corinth? What was Apollos' relationship? His role?
- When Paul says he laid the foundation, what does he mean? Who is the foundation? When do you think the foundation is laid? How does this relate to the metaphor of planting and watering?
- What do you think it means to build on the foundation?
    a. According to 1 Corinthians 3, what kind of materials can a person build with?
    b. Can a person produce gold, silver, or precious stones himself? Can he produce wood, hay, or straw (stubble)?
    c. Why do you think Paul uses these two different qualities of materials to make his point? How would a person get these materials? What would happen to each of these types of materials if you put them into a fire?
    d. Do you ever build on another person's foundation? Practically speaking, how would you do this? What would be God's Word to you in this regard?

- How does 1 Corinthians 3 relate to 1 Corinthians 4?
- What did you learn from marking the word *boast*[10] in these two chapters?
- Why would Paul possibly have to come to the Corinthians with a rod or whip? Does he have a right to do that? What gives him that right?
- What is the most significant thing you learned from this week's study? Have you changed any of your thinking or belief system? What about your behavior?
- How are you going to live in light of what you studied this week?

THOUGHT FOR THE WEEK

According to 1 Corinthians 3, you are fleshly (carnal or worldly) when you are caught in jealousy and strife or when you are a follower of men—choosing one teacher or man above another and lining yourself up with that particular person to the exclusion of others.

As I think of this passage, it seems to describe so many people in the church today. They can't take the solid food of the Word of God; instead, they need predigested milk. As it states in Hebrews 5:12-14: "For though by this time you ought to be teachers, you have need again for someone to teach you the elementary principles of the oracles of God, and you have come to need milk and not solid food. For everyone who partakes *only* of milk is not accustomed to the word of righteousness, for he is a babe. But solid food is for the mature, who because of practice have their senses trained to discern good and evil."

Because some haven't paid the price of time and discipline to study God's Word for themselves, they are babes and followers of men. Their doctrine comes from men, rather than from the Word of God. Therefore, they value one teacher above another, or pit one person's teaching against another's, without taking the time and making the effort to study God's Word for themselves.

When you don't study God's Word for yourself, when you don't take the time and make the effort to mine the treasures of God's Word—the gold, silver, and precious stones—then you can only share your opinions or your understanding of God's Word with others. Consequently you use what you produce rather than what you mine and discover, and in doing so you build with "wood, hay, and straw (or stubble)."

While your "building materials" may not be recognizable today, there is a day coming when what you verbalize to others—the advice you give, the counsel you share, the opinion you profess—will be judged by fire. What will be left of what you build in other people's lives after it's put in the fire?

You, Beloved, determine if you are willing to pay the price. If you are willing to "study to shew thyself ap-proved unto God, a workman that needeth not to be ashamed, rightly dividing the word of truth" (2 Timothy 2:15 KJV), your work will stand the fire. Remember, each of you is a steward of the mysteries of God (God's Word), and it's required that we be found faithful. So don't become arrogant. Don't boast (glory) in yourself. Don't boast (glory) in men. All things belong to you. Everything you have, you received from God! You're not superior—nor are you inferior! You are part of the family. Make sure you grow up and bring your heavenly Father joy.

WEEK THREE

What Do You Do When There's "Sin in the Camp"? Or in Your Own Life?

DAY ONE

Read 1 Corinthians 5 and mark every reference to the recipients. Think about the problem that is dealt with in this chapter.

DAY TWO

Read the fifth chapter again. This time mark every reference to Paul.

DAY THREE

Go through 1 Corinthians 5 again. Read it carefully and mark any key words. Check to see if you missed marking every reference to the recipients or to the author.

When you finish, add to your notebook lists everything you learn in this chapter about the Corinthians and about Paul.

On pages 70-71 is the chart THE FEASTS OF ISRAEL. If you have time you will find it profitable to study the first segment of the chart, "The 1st Month

(Nisan), Festival of Passover." It will help you understand Paul's reference to Christ, "our Passover," getting rid of the leaven (yeast) and keeping the feast with the unleavened bread of sincerity and truth.

DAY FOUR

Read 1 Corinthians 6 today. Mark every reference to the Corinthians.

Read chapter 6 again, and mark every reference to Paul and every occurrence of any of the key words on your bookmark. Also mark the word *body (bodies)*, but do not add it to your bookmark.

DAY FIVE

Read through 1 Corinthians 6 for a third time. Then add to your list what you learn about Paul and about the Corinthians. What seems to be the passions and relationships Paul is dealing with in this chapter and the previous one?

DAY SIX

Read Leviticus 20:10-21. Now read through 1 Corinthians 5 and 6 and mark every occurrence of the word *immoral*[11] or *immorality*.[12] Also mark the word *judge (judging, judges, judged)*.[13]

When you finish, list in your notebook everything you learn from these two chapters about immorality and the immoral. Don't add your opinion to the text; simply write down the facts of this chapter. Also, don't forget to record the themes of 1 Corinthians 5 and 6 on the 1 CORINTHIANS AT A GLANCE chart on page 72.

DAY SEVEN

Store in your heart: 1 Corinthians 6:9-11 or 6:19,20. (Preferably both!)

Read and discuss: 1 Corinthians 5:1-13; 6:9-20.

OPTIONAL QUESTIONS FOR DISCUSSION

- What is Paul's greatest concern in 1 Corinthians 5?
  - a. What was the attitude of the Corinthians in regard to the sin being committed by someone in the church?
  - b. How are the Corinthians described in chapter 5?
  - c. Do you think this same situation can be found in churches today? Discuss it.
- What were Paul's instructions to the Corinthians in 1 Corinthians 5?
  - a. What were they to do with the immoral man in their midst?
  - b. Why were they to do this? State all the reasons: i.e., for the individual man and for the church as a body.
  - c. What is leaven (yeast) and how does it work in dough?

d. What does Paul mean when he says, "Christ our Passover also has been sacrificed"? To what is Paul alluding? Discuss what you learned from the "Feasts of Israel" chart.

e. Who is the church to judge? Who are they not to judge? Look at every place you marked the word *judge* and its forms in 1 Corinthians 5 and 6 and discuss what you learned.

❧ What did you learn from marking the words *immoral*[14] and *immorality*[15] in these two chapters? Make sure you don't miss anything Paul says about immorality in 1 Corinthians 5 and 6.

a. Discuss what happens when a Christian is immoral: What does it do to Christ? According to this passage, can immorality be the continuous lifestyle of a Christian? Can a Christian be immoral? Can he live in habitual immorality as a professing Christian and still hope for heaven? You may want to compare this passage with Galatians 5:19-21 and Ephesians 5:3-5.

b. What is Paul's basis for telling the Christians that they should not be involved in immorality? Discuss what you learned from marking every occurrence of the word *body* or *bodies.*

c. How needful do you think this message is for the church today and why?

d. What would you say to a person who claims to be a Christian, a "so-called brother or sister," who is living in immorality? What should be your response and your relationship to this person? On what basis?

- How has God spoken to your heart in respect to these chapters?
  a. Is there anyone in the church that you need to deal with? How will you do it? (You may want to look at Matthew 18:15-20.)
  b. What are you doing with your body, God's temple—His Holy of Holies?

THOUGHT FOR THE WEEK

O Beloved, is there immorality among you? Why are you tolerating it? Is it because you excuse it as a weakness of the flesh, a weakness that anyone is susceptible to?

Mourn! Don't tolerate it in the arrogance of your human reasoning or logic. Sin, like leaven, spreads. It will have its effect on the church. It will give the world a covering—a cloak with which to cover its sin.

Judge the sin. Shut out the sinners if there's no repentance, so that they might feel the awfulness of their sin and return to the Lord. Or else they will experience the awful devastation it will take upon their flesh as they sin against their own bodies.

Don't deem yourself wiser than God. Listen to Him and do what He says—He has already judged the situation. It is written in 1 Corinthians 5 and 6. And remember, Beloved, that your body is His temple and you are not to take the members of your body—your eyes, hands, etc., and use them for immoral acts. Your body is no longer your own; it is a temple for God. His Shekinah glory dwells there in the form of the Holy Spirit. Determine that everything in His temple will say glory to the Lord.

Remember the price that was paid that you might be His. Jesus Christ, the Passover Lamb, was sacrificed for you. Keep the feast!

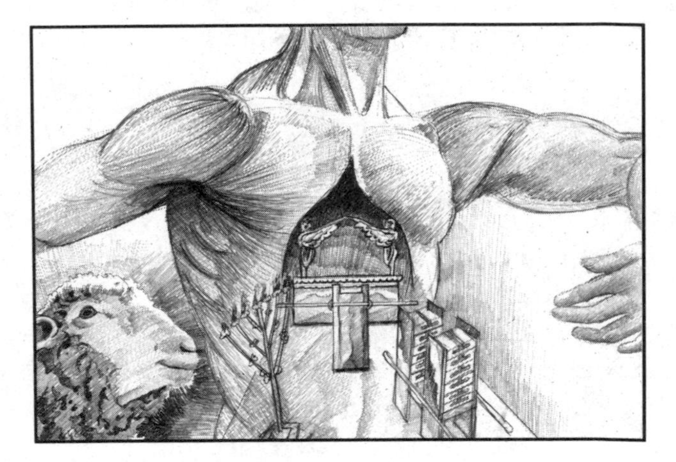

Week Four

What About Singleness, Sexuality . . . or Being Married to an Unbeliever?

Day One

Read through 1 Corinthians 7 to familiarize yourself with the content of the chapter. Note how the chapter begins. Remember, this chapter marks the next segment of Paul's epistle to the Corinthians. Having dealt with certain problems in the church, he now turns to their questions regarding specific issues.

As you read, mark every reference to being married: i.e., *marriage,*[16] *married, marries, marry, bound.*

We will only deal with 1 Corinthians 7 this week. It is a long and important chapter that has much to say about marriage and is pertinent to today.

Day Two

Read through 1 Corinthians 7:1-7 today. Mark the references to the Corinthians and to Paul. Also mark the words *immoralities*[17] and *body*.

When you finish, once again list in your notebook what you learn about Paul. It is interesting. Also list anything you learn about the Corinthians.

Then, either in your notebook or in the margin of your Bible, list what God says regarding the husband's and the wife's responsibility in respect to their bodies and their sexual responsibility to one another. Also note why there is a responsibility.

According to this passage, why should a man or woman consider marriage? Think about what you read and what it implies regarding alternative ways to meet one's sexual needs.

DAY THREE

Read 1 Corinthians 7:8-16. Mark the words *unbeliever*[18] or *unbelieving.*[19] Then in your notebook make a list of God's instructions through Paul to the following people: unmarried, widows, wives, husbands, and the unbelieving.

When you finish, think about all these short verses teach in respect to marriage and living with or departing from the unbelieving mate. Remember that this is the Word of God and we need to listen to it very carefully so we will know how we are to live.

DAY FOUR

Read 1 Corinthians 7:17-24. Mark every occurrence of the word *called.*[20] Note what Paul is referring to when he speaks of our being called. Note, too, the different states people can find themselves in when they are "called" and what they are to do in respect to these states or conditions of life. Make notes on all you learn about being called in your notebook.

DAY FIVE

Read 1 Corinthians 7:25-40 and mark every occurrence of the word *virgin(s)*. Also note how verse 25 begins in respect to 7:1.

List in your notebook everything God says regarding virgins. Remember that when this chapter was written, marriages were arranged by the parents—the father in particular.

DAY SIX

Read 1 Corinthians 7:17-40 again. This time mark the word *concern(ed)*.[21] Also mark every occurrence of the words *husband* and *wife* and every reference to the Corinthians.

Then look at 1 Corinthians 7:26-28. Remember, Paul has been talking about remaining in the state in which you were called (saved). What then is his instruction to those who are bound (married) and to those who have been released (divorced)?[22]

Mark any references to Paul. Don't forget to add these insights to your list and also add insights on the recipients to that list.

Now look at 1 Corinthians 7:29-35 and note what God's exhortation is for those who are married. If you are married, does this apply to you? How does it fit with everything you have been taught regarding marriage?

List in your notebook all you learn from 1 Corinthians 7:17-40 in respect to husbands and to wives.

Record the theme of 1 Corinthians 7 on the 1 CORINTHIANS AT A GLANCE chart.

DAY SEVEN

Store in your heart: If you are single, memorize 1 Corinthians 7:1,2. If you are married, memorize 1 Corinthians 7:5. If you are in a difficult marriage, memorize 1 Corinthians 7:10,11.

Read and discuss: 1 Corinthians 7. (It's good to read the entire chapter to give the class the context. If you are all using the same version of the Bible [NAS, NIV, KJV, or NKJV], it would be good for the class to read it aloud.)

OPTIONAL QUESTIONS FOR DISCUSSION

- Do you see any connection between what Paul says regarding immorality in 1 Corinthians 6 and what he says about immorality in 1 Corinthians 7? Explain.
    a. According to 1 Corinthians, what is the solution for those who cannot live a single life and remain sexually pure? Where does this place sexual self-satisfaction (masturbation) as an option for meeting a person's sexual needs?
    b. In light of what you shared in "a." what is the husband's and the wife's sexual responsibility to each other?

c. Does this provide any guidelines or set any precedent in respect to a couple living together even though they are not married?

- What do you learn about Paul's marital status?
- As you carefully observed this chapter, what did you learn from the Word of God (remember it *is* God's Word) regarding the following:

  a. those who are married to unbelievers

  b. the children of those married to unbelievers

  c. the state we are in when we are saved in respect to what we are to do once we are saved

  d. those who are released (divorced from a mate)

  e. those who are bound (married) when they are saved

  f. virgins

- What is God's ideal? According to 1 Corinthians 7:32, what does God want? Why?
- How long is a person to be married (bound)? How would 1 Corinthians 7:39 compare with what was stated previously in 1 Corinthians 7:15,16?*
- What have you learned from your personal study of this chapter? What insights have you gleaned? How do they compare with what you have been taught?

*If you want to do a more thorough and comprehensive study of the subject of marriage, divorce, and remarriage, so that you see for yourself what the Scriptures say, then order the inductive study course *Marriage Without Regrets.* For information on this course, call or write: Precept Ministries, P.O. Box 182218, Chattanooga, TN, 37422, (615) 892-6814.

ೂ What do you know that you should do in light of this information? Will you?

THOUGHT FOR THE WEEK

When you find yourself in a difficult situation, seeking a way out, do you turn to people to get counsel that will help you *out of* your predicament? It's hard to believe that God would want you unhappy or uncomfortable, isn't it?

What you might want to consider is the fact that God wants you to be holy even as He is holy. You are to be set apart, different from ordinary people—people who don't know God and are devoid of the Holy Spirit of God.

Don't forget that the Lord Himself says in Jeremiah 17:5-10, "Cursed is the man who trusts in mankind and makes flesh his strength, and whose heart turns away from the LORD. For he will be like a bush in the desert and will not see when prosperity comes, but will live in stony wastes in the wilderness, a land of salt without inhabitant. Blessed is the man who trusts in the LORD and whose trust is the LORD. For he will be like a tree planted by the water, that extends its roots by a stream and will not fear when the heat comes; but its leaves will be green, and it will not be anxious in a year of drought nor cease to yield fruit. The heart is more deceitful than all else and is desperately sick; who can understand it? I, the LORD, search the heart, I test the mind, even to give to each man according to his ways, according to the results of his deeds."

How crucial—how imperative—it is to your ultimate welfare and happiness that you seek God's counsel in His

Word and then walk in His ways, rather than according to your own desires, reasoning, or rationalizing.

You have seen very clearly what God says to the married and to the unmarried. You have seen what He says about your sexuality and what He says about living with an unbeliever. You have also seen what He says to those who have been deserted, to those who were saved after they were divorced, to those who are married, and to those who have been widowed.

Will you listen? To listen is not merely to hear, but to obey. Choose obedience and you choose life. God, by His Spirit, will enable you to do what He has called you to do. Then, Beloved, when you see Him you won't be ashamed. You'll be applauded and rewarded.

WEEK FIVE

How Do You Relate to Christians Who Hold Different Views on Certain Issues?

DAY ONE

Read 1 Corinthians 8. As you do, note that Paul is now going to deal with a new subject: things sacrificed to idols. Therefore, read this chapter and mark every reference to *idol(s)* in a distinctive way. Then add *idol(s)* and its synonym, *idolatry*, to your bookmark.

When you finish your marking, list in your notebook everything you learn. As you do, you will see some interesting things connected with idols.

DAY TWO

Yesterday, as you listed all you learned regarding idols, you observed that the food offered to idols was sold in restaurants in the idol's temple (8:10). In other words, there was a food business on the side—apparently the sacrifices were not thrown away once they were offered to idols. Instead they were sold as food!

Now, the question was, What about this? Could believers in Christ eat food sacrificed to idols? As you observe the text you will discover not only Paul's answer, but, at the same time, you will gain insight into how you are to deal with a weaker brother. Read through 1 Corinthians 8 again. This time mark every reference to the author as you have done before. Also mark every reference to the Corinthians, the recipients. However, if the author includes the recipients (the Corinthians) in the pronouns "we" or "us," then combine the colors you use for the author and for the recipients so you can see what Paul is doing as he identifies himself with the Corinthians.

Also mark the key word *knowledge*.

When you finish, list in your notebook what you learn about knowledge and what you learn from marking every reference in which Paul refers to himself and to the recipients as "we" or "us."

DAY THREE

Read through 1 Corinthians 8 again. Mark every occurrence of the word *weak*. When you finish, read the chapter again and this time mark any other words that would also be references to "the weak," i.e., *brother*.

Then list everything you learn about the weak. Think about who Paul considers weak and why.

Finally, add to your list everything you marked yesterday about the recipients from Paul's direct references to them.

DAY FOUR

Read 1 Corinthians 9 and mark every reference to Paul so you can add these to your list. As you read, see if Paul mentions idols or idolatry in this chapter. If so, mark it.

DAY FIVE

Read 1 Corinthians 9 again. Mark key words and be sure not to miss marking *gospel* and *boast.*[23] Also mark every occurrence of *weak* and *Law.*[24]

Again, mark any reference to the recipients of this epistle.

When you finish, list in your notebook everything you learn from marking the word *gospel.*

DAY SIX

Read through 1 Corinthians 9 again.

Although there is no reference to idols or idolatry in this chapter, Paul is not finished with the subject of things sacrificed to idols. Next week we will see what else he has to say about this subject in chapter 10. However, at this point we need to stop and think about why Paul says what he says in chapter 9. What point is he trying to make?

Record the themes of 1 Corinthians 8 and 9 on the 1 CORINTHIANS AT A GLANCE chart.

DAY SEVEN

Store in your heart: 1 Corinthians 9:19,22.
Read and discuss: Romans 14:1,2,13-23.

OPTIONAL QUESTIONS FOR DISCUSSION

Before we discuss the practical value of these chapters, let's discuss what we learned this week as we studied 1 Corinthians 8 and 9.

- What did you learn about idols from 1 Corinthians 8? What is the knowledge that Paul and the Corinthians had regarding idols?
- From what you observed in 1 Corinthians 8, describe who Paul refers to as "the weak".
- What is to be our attitude and/or response to those brothers and sisters who fall into the category of "weak"? As you answer this question, remember what Paul says in 1 Corinthians 9 regarding the weak.
- How does what Paul says regarding the weak correspond with what is taught in Romans 14:1,2,13-23?
- Since Paul is not finished with the subject of eating things sacrificed to idols (he will mention it again in chapter 10), what relationship do you think chapter 9 has to chapter 8?
- What do you learn about Paul in 1 Corinthians 8 and 9?

  a. Why do you suppose Paul says what he says in the beginning of 1 Corinthians 9?

b. What was Paul's attitude toward preaching the gospel?

c. What extent did Paul go to—what position did he take—in order to reach others? What different classes or groups of people are mentioned in 1 Corinthians 9:19-23?

d. What place did Paul give to his own personal preferences and his liberty in Christ?

❧ If there are no heathen temples around you, nor stores or restaurants that sell food that has been offered to idols, do the chapters that you studied this week have anything to say to you?

a. If yes, what?

b. What principles or precepts do you see in these chapters that can help you live a more Christlike life?

c. What do you see as your responsibility or relationship to the gospel?

❧ What do you learn from 1 Corinthians 9 regarding the believer's responsibility to those who minister the Word (the gospel)? How well do you fulfill this responsibility?

THOUGHT FOR THE WEEK

In an age when the general or overriding philosophy centers around self—taking care of self, pleasing self, seeing the worth of self, and the importance of doing that which will help us respect self and achieve our full potential as a human being and will make "us" happy—the teaching of 1 Corinthians 8 and 9 can easily be rationalized away or ignored.

Yet, Beloved, was not our Lord's word very clear? "If anyone wishes to come after Me, let him deny himself, and take up his cross, and follow Me. For whoever wishes to save his life shall lose it; but whoever loses his life for My sake and the gospel's shall save it" (Mark 8:34,35).

In 1 Corinthians 8 and 9 Paul demonstrates the practical outworkings of a crucified life as he reminds you that, although Christ has set you free from all men, you are to become their slaves that you might win them to Christ (1 Corinthians 9:19-21). However, this submission of self is not only to reach the lost, but, out of love, to subjugate self even to the brethren, to not flaunt your liberty so that it becomes a stumbling block to those still weak in faith.

Everything Paul did was for the sake of the gospel. Oh, my friend, can you imagine what would happen first in the church, and then in the world, if everyone who named the name of Christ did the same as Paul did? What would happen if you buffeted your body and made it your slave, instead of being its slave?

Think on these things. According to Paul, and, thus, to the Word of God, if you don't live this way, you disqualify yourself. Remember, the cross is the pivotal point of Christianity.

Week Six

How Do You Handle Your Cravings, Your Temptations?

Day One

Chapter and verse divisions are manmade, therefore you cannot assume that each time you come to another chapter in the Bible, you come to another subject. As you begin this week's study, read 1 Corinthians 9:19–10:33, through without stopping. When you come to 10:31-33 note how these verses correspond with 9:19-27 as you see Paul's heart for the sake of the gospel.

Now then, read through 1 Corinthians 10 again. Watch the continuation of Paul's thought from 9:24-27 into 10:1. Note the "For" in 10:1.[25] As you read, mark every reference to Paul and to the recipients as you have done previously. If you come to a "we" or "us" that includes Paul with the Corinthians, don't forget to combine the colors you are using to show that the pronoun includes both groups.

Day Two

Read 1 Corinthians 10:1-13. Watch for the reference to the *fathers*.[26] Be sure to note every occurrence of the word *all* when it refers to the word *fathers.* Note what "all" did, but also note how God felt about most of them.

Mark any reference to *idols* or *idolaters.* Also mark the word *example(s).*[27]

Read 1 Corinthians 10:7 to look at the first of these examples. Then note what the people did and read Exodus 32:1-8,15-28. Remember, these were people who experienced the same things as described in 1 Corinthians 10:1-4, but 3000 of them were put to death. Examine this incident recorded in Exodus in the light of the 5 W's and an H: Who put them to death? Why were they put to death? What did they do? When did they do it? Where were they? and How were they put to death?

Since these are examples, you need to examine your life in light of what you learn.

DAY THREE

Today, continue looking at the examples listed in 1 Corinthians 10:7-10. Read 1 Corinthians 10:8 and then Numbers 25:1-9. Note the reference to immorality. Has Paul dealt with immorality before in his epistle to the Corinthians?

Now read 1 Corinthians 10:9 and compare it with Numbers 21:4-9.

Finally, read 1 Corinthians 10:10 and then look up the following passages in Numbers: 14:1-4,11,12,26-30; and chapter 16. As you read, mark the references to *grumble* or *grumbled*[28] in a distinctive way and then note what happened to those who grumbled. If you have time, it would be profitable to read Numbers 17:1-11.

Did you see the correlation between the verses in 1 Corinthians and those in Numbers? Write the verses which correlate to one another as cross-references, close to the appropriate text in 1 Corinthians, in the margin of your Bible. Cross-referencing helps when you may not remember the location of a passage that sheds light on or correlates with the one you are studying. Cross-referencing is also very helpful when you do not have your study notes because your notes are right in your Bible!

DAY FOUR

Remembering what you studied the last three days and the subject Paul began in 1 Corinthians 8:1, read 1 Corinthians 10:14-33. Mark every reference to *idols* and *idolatry*. Also mark every occurrence of the word *demons*.[29] If you are marking every reference to the devil in a particular way, then mark *demons* the same way. If you don't already have a symbol to use, you may want to mark these references with a pitchfork as I do, like this: **devil**.

Also, in a distinctive way mark every occurrence of the word *conscience*.

When you finish, note the connection between idols and demons. Also make a list in your notebook from what you learn by marking the word *conscience*.

DAY FIVE

Read 1 Corinthians 11:1-17. Note how 1 Corinthians 11:1 relates to what was just said in 1 Corinthians 10.

As you read 1 Corinthians 11:1-16, mark in distinctive ways the references to the woman and the references to the man, then in your notebook list everything you learn from marking each of these words in this text.

DAY SIX

Read 1 Corinthians 11:2 and note why Paul praises them. Then read 11:17-34 and note what Paul **cannot** praise them about. Mark every occurrence of the word *praise* in this passage. Also go back to 1 Corinthians 11:2 and mark the word *praise*.

Also mark every occurrence of the word *judge (judged, judgment)*.[30] Remember to mark it the same way you did when you studied 1 Corinthians 5 and 6.

Be sure not to miss marking the word *divisions* in this passage.

When you finish reading and marking these words, think about why Paul could not praise them, and record it in your notebook. Note what the Lord's Supper is all about, how they were behaving, what was happening as a result of their behavior, and what God wanted them to do, and why. Apply what you learn to your own behavior in respect to taking "the Lord's Supper" or "Holy Communion."

Record the themes of 1 Corinthians 10 and 11 on the 1 CORINTHIANS AT A GLANCE chart.

DAY SEVEN

Store in your heart: 1 Corinthians 10:13.
Read and discuss: 1 Corinthians 10:1-22.

OPTIONAL QUESTIONS FOR DISCUSSION

- Paul began dealing with the subject of eating things offered to idols in 1 Corinthians 8. What does Paul seem to be stressing to the Corinthians in 1 Corinthians 10:1-22 regarding idols? What did you learn from this passage?
- Sometimes people want to simply combine "Christ" or "Christianity" with their former lifestyle or beliefs. They want to believe on Christ or adopt Christianity and then go back to their former lifestyle or beliefs whenever it is convenient or seemingly advantageous. From all that you studied this week, is this possible?
    a. Discuss what you learned from the Old Testament cross-references you looked up as you studied 1 Corinthians 10:7-10.
    b. How were these incidents in the life of Israel examples as 1 Corinthians 10:6,11 says? Discuss what situations these might parallel in society today.
    c. Discuss God's warning in 1 Corinthians 10:12 and His promise in 10:13. The greek word for temptation is *peirasmos* and means "a trial, temptation, putting to the test, a trial of one's character, a state of trial."

- According to 1 Corinthians 10:16-22, why is it impossible to share in the body and blood of Christ and participate in idolatry?
- Under what conditions could a person eat something offered to idols? Why?
  a. If people were allowed to eat something offered to idols, why couldn't they participate in idolatry?
  b. In light of all this, can a person live on both sides of the fence in respect to Christianity? (If there is time, you may also want to discuss chapter 11, especially what you learn from this passage about taking the Lord's Supper [Holy Communion.])
- What is the significance of taking the Lord's Supper?
  a. What are you remembering when you take communion?
  b. According to this chapter, what was Christ's purpose in dying?
  c. If Christ died for your sins, and you are taking the Lord's Supper while you are sinning or you have no intention of dealing with that sin and forsaking it, what can you expect according to this passage?
  d. Is it fair?
  e. What did you learn from marking the word *judge* and its synonyms?
  f. What did you learn from this passage that you need to remember when you take the Lord's Supper or Holy Communion?

~ How has God personally spoken to you through this week's study?

THOUGHT FOR THE WEEK

Beloved, you have God's promise. No matter what trial, testing, or temptation comes your way, God has provided His way of escape. Not yours, but His. Therefore you *can* behave righteously. You *can* do what God says is right, no matter the magnitude of the trial or the temptation. Your situation is not unique; others have been tempted or tested in the same way. They also have either walked away victorious or have come away defeated according to whether or not they listened to and obeyed God.

Remember, people can go through all sorts of experiences with God, even as the children of Israel did when they left Egypt, crossed the Red Sea on dry ground, ate manna, and drank water from the rock. You can see and experience God's power and deliverance, but this means nothing in the eyes of God if you don't live the way a true child of God is to live. Don't rely only on your experiences with God or with Christianity. Christianity is a total commitment to God and that commitment is seen in your day-by-day relationship with Him, a life committed to Him alone.

Christianity is not something you add to what you already believe. Rather, it is a total identification with Christ, with His body, and, thus, a separation from all else. You cannot share the cup of the Lord and the cup of demons. God is a jealous God. His name is *Qanna*—Jealous—and He will not allow you to worship any other god but Him. Remember that and choose you this day whom you will serve.

Week Seven

What About Spiritual Gifts and Those Who Have What You Don't?

Day One

Paul now addresses the next subject he needs to cover with the Corinthians. Read 1 Corinthians 12:1 and note his subject. It is what we will study this week as we cover 1 Corinthians 12, 13, and 14.

Read through Chapters 12–14. Mark every direct reference to Paul and to the Corinthians as you have done throughout the book. Also, in a distinctive way, mark every occurrence of the word *gifts*. Also mark the word *division*[31] as you have marked it before.

When you finish, read 1 Corinthians 1:4-10. Mark any reference to *gifts* in this passage and also note the use of the word *divisions*.[32]

Now look at the places where you marked references to Paul and to the Corinthians. In your notebook, record Paul's concerns in these three chapters. Also list what you learn about Paul and the recipients.

Day Two

Read through 1 Corinthians 12 today. Remember—if

you read aloud it will help you remember what you read. As you read be sure to mark every reference to the *Holy Spirit*[33] including all pronouns.

When you finish, record everything you learn from chapter 12 about the Holy Spirit.

DAY THREE

Today, read through 1 Corinthians 12 again. This time focus on the various gifts Paul mentions in this chapter. List these gifts in your notebook. Also list everything you learn about gifts in general from this chapter. Use the 5 W's and an H: Who gets these gifts? What are the gifts? How does a person get these gifts? When does he get them? How many does he get? Think about what you learned from marking every reference to the Holy Spirit yesterday.

DAY FOUR

Read 1 Corinthians 12 one more time. This time we are going to focus on the analogy Paul uses in explaining the giving of the gifts and their individual importance. As you read Chapter 12, mark every occurrence of the word *body* and the word *member(s)*.[34] As you mark these words —each in its own distinctive way—note the relationship of the members to the body and how Paul compares these to spiritual gifts. What are the gifts likened to? What is Paul trying to achieve through this analogy?

DAY FIVE

Read 1 Corinthians 13 and mark the following key words in a distinctive way: *tongues, prophecy (prophesy),*[35] and *love.*[36] Then go back to 1 Corinthians 12:10,28,30 and mark in the same way each occurrence of the word *tongues.*

When you finish reading this chapter and marking the key words, note what Paul is saying and why. Keep in mind all you have observed this week.

DAY SIX

Read 1 Corinthians 14 today. Mark the following key words: *prophesy (prophesies, prophecy, prophet, prophets), tongue(s),* and *edifies (edification, edifying, edified).*[37] Don't forget to mark synonyms.

When you finish, list in your notebook everything 1 Corinthians 12–14 teaches regarding tongues.

Now mark the word *prophecy* and *prophets* in 1 Corinthians 12:10,28,29 and then list everything chapters 12–14 teach regarding the gift of prophecy.

Finally, look at every reference you marked for *edification* and its forms and list in your notebook what you learn.

Record the themes of 1 Corinthians 12, 13, and 14 on your AT A GLANCE chart.

DAY SEVEN

Store in your heart: 1 Corinthians 12:13,18 or 1 Corinthians 12:4-7.

Read and discuss: 1 Corinthians 12:4-31; 1 Peter 4:10.

OPTIONAL QUESTIONS FOR DISCUSSION

- What is 1 Corinthians 12–14 about and why, from your observations of this text, do you think Paul had to deal with this subject? Be as thorough in your answer as you can be, noting what Paul emphasizes in chapters 13 and 14.
- What did you learn regarding spiritual gifts from studying these chapters? For instance:
  - a. Who gives the gifts?
  - b. To whom are they given?
  - c. On what basis?
  - d. What is their purpose?
  - e. When are the gifts given?
  - f. Are any gifts more important than others?
  - g. What gifts should a body of believers, a church, desire? Why?
- Why does Paul use the analogy of the human body when he explains spiritual gifts? What can we learn from this analogy that will help us appreciate others?
- What did you learn from these chapters about:
  - a. tongues?
  - b. prophecy?
- Why do you think Paul brings up the subject of love (charity) in 1 Corinthians 13? What point is he trying to make? Why was it necessary?
- Read 1 Corinthians 12:4-6 carefully. Note the word *varieties*[38] and then note what there are varieties of.

Also note what member of the Godhead is connected with each variety. How do verses 7 and 11 tie in with verse 4 and the gifts and the Spirit?

- What do you learn from 1 Peter 4:10?
- What have you learned about spiritual gifts that you can apply to your own life? Do you have a spiritual gift? Do you know what it is? Do you know your responsibility toward this gift?*

THOUGHT FOR THE WEEK

O Beloved, were you aware that when you believed on the Lord Jesus Christ the Holy Spirit not only came to indwell you but He gave you one or more spiritual gifts?

Have there been times when you wondered why on earth God saved you or what His purpose was for your life? Now you can rest assured that faithful is He who called you, who will also do it! God never calls you to a task that He has not already gifted you to accomplish. You are, as Ephesians 2:10 says, "his workmanship, created in Christ Jesus unto good works, which God hath before ordained that [you] should walk in them" (KJV). Therefore, when you were saved (as 1 Corinthians 12:18 says), God placed you as a member in the body of Christ exactly where it pleased Him. You were created *by* God and *for* God. God has a plan, a purpose for your life.

---

*Precept Ministries has an inductive sutdy course called *Spiritual Gifts*. If you would like more information on that course, or any of our other study courses, write or call Precept Ministries, P.O. Box 182218, Chattanooga, TN, 37422, (615) 892-6814.

Every child of God has been gifted by God. Although the gifts vary, and the ministry varies, and the effect varies, you are vital to God and to the church of the Lord Jesus Christ. You have been given your gifts for the common good of the church, for the edifying of the body of Christ.

Therefore, Beloved, ask God to show you what your gifts are. I believe the way to discover your gifts is not by taking the manmade tests that some have written, but to ask God to show you what your gifts are. As you step forward, making yourself available to God for whatever He pleases, He will lead you. You will discover your gifts much as you would a natural talent. You will be drawn to them. And when you are exercising your gifts, you will experience confirmation from the Spirit and from other people as they are edified because you are operating in the realm of the Spirit.

Remember you are a steward of your gifts. They were given to you for a purpose—so exercise them for the benefit of others. But remember to always do it in love for apart from love your gifts are useless.

Don't be jealous of the gifts of others. God gave you what He wanted you to have. Also remember you are not accountable to be or do what others do. You are accountable only for your gifts and ministry. Don't look at the effects and evaluate yourself or your gifts on that basis. Gifts are from the Spirit, the ministry from the Lord, and the effect is from God—your responsibility is simply to be faithful. If you have a speaking gift, speak the utterances of God. If you have a serving gift, serve in the strength that God provides so that in all things God will be glorified through Jesus Christ, to whom belongs the glory and dominion forever and ever.

Week Eight

What's the Gospel I'm to Live By and Preach . . . and Why?

Day One

Having concluded what he has to say regarding spiritual gifts, Paul turns to another subject. Read 1 Corinthians 15 and note that subject. Mark every reference to Paul, to the Corinthians, and don't miss marking any occurrence of the word *gospel* (along with its synonyms). As you mark the references to the Corinthians, you will see why Paul had to deal with the subject of the resurrection. Add any new insights you learned to your lists in your notebook.

Day Two

Read through 1 Corinthians 15:1-11. Mark every reference to Jesus Christ, including pronouns. Make a bookmark for this chapter adding to it each key word as it is given to you. Then look for and mark these key words throughout the week. As you look for the key words, don't miss any pronouns or synonyms, especially in reference to Christ. (Later on He will be referred to as the "last Adam" and that you don't want to miss.)

Now read verses 1-11 again. This time mark the word *preach(ed)* and *delivered*[39] in the same way. Also underline or mark in another way the phrase *according to the Scriptures*. Then, in your notebook, list the points of what was preached (delivered) and how what was preached was verified.

DAY THREE

Read 1 Corinthians 15:1-34 and mark *death*. Be sure to mark every form, i.e.: *die, died, the dead, fallen asleep, asleep*.[40]

Also mark every occurrence of the word *raise(d)* and *resurrection*,[41] and mark the key words from your bookmark. Then look at each reference to *raise*d or *resurrection* and ask the 5 W's and an H: What is happening? Who is raised? How? When? Why? Where? Watch Paul's reasoning regarding the resurrection carefully to see why it is such an important issue.

Remember that some people in the church at Corinth were saying that there is no resurrection of the dead (verse 12). Think about the message of the gospel as defined in 15:1-11.

Read Romans 4:25, then stop and think about what the resurrection shows in respect to our sin.

Record in your notebook everything you learn from this passage about Christ being raised and the dead being raised.

DAY FOUR

Read 1 Corinthians 15:35-49. Note the question Paul begins with in verse 35 and then how he proceeds to answer the question. As you read, mark the words *body* and *bodies*.

Also watch Paul's references to the first and last Adam, the first man and the second man. Mark every reference to Jesus Christ, including all synonyms.

DAY FIVE

Read 1 Corinthians 15:50-58 and mark key words. (You marked *death* and its forms on Day Three. Verses 50-58 (KJV) use another synonym of this key word—*grave*. Be sure not to miss marking it.) Watch for the word *mystery* and note what the mystery is.

Give careful attention to what ultimately happens to death and why. Also note the ultimate conclusion of this chapter and God's message to you.

Finally, read through this vital fifteenth chapter again, watching every place you have marked the references to Christ. In your notebook list all you learn from this chapter about Him. It will take a little time, but it will be worth it.

DAY SIX

Read the final chapter of 1 Corinthians today. Note the final subject Paul covers in 1 Corinthians 16. Mark every reference to Paul and to the recipients as you have done throughout this book. Also mark the word *love*[42] and any reference to the Lord. Add any new insights about Jesus Christ to your lists. When you finish, note what you learn about love and the Lord, and ask yourself how you measure up. You also might want to look at verse 13 and take it as a personal word. Compare the phrase *act like men*[43] with 3:1; 14:20. Surely all the studying you have done in this course confirms to you that you are going on to maturity, acting like men rather than babes. You are to be congratulated.

Record the theme of 1 Corinthians 15 and 16 on the AT A GLANCE chart. Then stop and think through the book of Corinthians. Note what chapters form a segment of truth, a particular theme, and record this on the chart under segment divisions.

DAY SEVEN

Store in your heart: 1 Corinthians 15:10 or 1 Corinthians 15: 1,2.

Read and discuss: 1 Corinthians 15:1-26.

OPTIONAL QUESTIONS FOR DISCUSSION

- According to 1 Corinthians 15:3-8, what are the main points of the Gospel and what is the evidence of their reality? (Looking at the repeated phrase "according to the Scriptures" will show you the two main points of the Gospel.)

- Discuss: If there is **no** resurrection, then . . .
  - a. where do we stand?
  - b. what about Jesus?
  - c. what about our faith?
  - d. how should we live and why? (Have the class support these answers with Scripture.)
- In 1 Corinthians 15 Paul refers to us as being in Adam or in Christ. What is the end result of each association? Why do you think Paul refers to Christ as the last Adam in 15:45?
- What is the order of the resurrection? If there is time, you might also want to discuss what you learned about our resurrection bodies.
- When will death finally be totally conquered? Look at 15:26,54-56 and compare it with Revelation 20:5,6, 11-14.
- What do you think Paul is saying in 1 Corinthians 15:1,2? What is the point he is trying to get across?
- In 1 Corinthians 15:58, Paul says our toil (labor) is not in vain. Why isn't it?
- What has God said to you in this week of study?
- What was the most significant, life-changing truth you learned in your study of 1 Corinthians? How are you going to live as a result of this study?

THOUGHT FOR THE WEEK

Someday, you are going to bear the image of the heavenly—the image of our Lord Jesus Christ. Remember that and stay alert. Don't become complacent in your Christianity or lax in your walk with the Lord. Don't become caught up in worldly wisdom, in empty boasting. Put away divisions and quarrels and remember that you are part of Christ's body, one member among many but placed there according to God's will and purpose for you.

There is so much for you to learn! Move from milk to meat—don't stay a babe in Christ. And don't excuse sin in your own life or in the life of the church. Remember, Christ your Passover has been sacrificed for you, so celebrate the feast by walking in sincerity—a genuineness of faith—and in truth.

Remember, your body is part of Christ's body. Therefore, don't let any member of Christ's body be involved in any form of immorality—not even in your thought life. Be content with the mate to whom you are married and, if you are single, remain pure or get married. Remember that, because the coming of the Lord is near, you should serve Him with undistracted devotion.

Examine your life. Have you set up any idols in your heart? Don't provoke the Lord to jealousy. He is to be your all in all. And if He is, then you will live for the sake of the gospel and not for the comfort or pleasure of self. You will not flaunt your liberty in Christ, but you will become all things to all men in order that you might win some to Christ. You will do all things for the sake of the gospel. So bring your body into subjection; make it your slave. Remember that no temptation will overtake you that God will not provide you a way of escape.

Every time you partake of the Lord's Supper, you are remembering that He died to deliver you from sin. Don't take the bread or drink of the cup if you are not willing to judge any sin in your life and put it away. Otherwise, God will have to judge you, if you don't judge yourself (1 Corinthians 11:28–32).

Remember the Gospel. It is only effective for salvation if you hold fast to it. Just to say you believe it but not live accordingly is to "believe in vain." True salvation is confirmed by a changed life. "Or do you not know that the unrighteous shall not inherit the kingdom of God? Do not be deceived; neither fornicators, nor idolaters, nor adulterers, nor effeminate, nor homosexuals, nor thieves, nor the covetous, nor drunkards, nor revilers, nor swindlers, shall inherit the kingdom of God. And such were some of you; but you were washed, but you were sanctified, but you were justified in the name of the Lord Jesus Christ, and in the Spirit of our God" (1 Corinthians 6:9-11). So "be on the alert, stand firm in the faith, act like men, be strong. Let all that you do be done in love" (1 Corinthians 16:13,14).

The Feasts of Israel

	1st Month (Nisan) Festival of Passover				3rd Month (Sivan) Festival of Pentecost
Slaves in Egypt	**Passover**	**Unleavened Bread**	**Firstfruits**		**Pentecost or Feast of Weeks**

	Kill lamb & put blood on doorpost Exodus 12:6, 7	***Purging of all leaven*** (symbol of sin)	***Wave offering of sheaf*** (promise of harvest to come)		***Wave offering of two loaves of leavened bread***
	1st month, 14th day Leviticus 23:5	1st month, 15th day for 7 days Leviticus 23:6-8	Day after Sabbath Leviticus 23:9-14		50 days after firstfruits Leviticus 23:15-21
Whosoever commits sin is the slave to sin	**Christ our Passover has been sacrificed** 	**Clean out old leaven... just as you are in fact unleavened**	**Christ has been raised...the firstfruits** 	**Going away so Comforter can come**  **Mount of Olives**	**Promise of the Spirit, mystery of church: Jews-Gentiles in one body** 
John 8:34	1 Corinthians 5:7	1 Corinthians 5:7, 8	1 Corinthians 15:20-23	John 16:7 Acts 1:9-12	Acts 2:1-47 1 Corinthians 12:13 Ephesians 2:11-22

Months: Nisan—*March, April* • **Sivan**—*May, June* • **Tishri**—*September, October*

	7th Month (Tishri) Festival of Tabernacles			
	Feast of Trumpets 	**Day of Atonement** 	**Feast of Booths or Tabernacles** 	
Interlude Between Festivals	*Trumpet blown — a holy convocation*	*Atonement shall be made to cleanse you* Leviticus 16:30	*Harvest celebration memorial of tabernacles in wilderness*	
	7th month, 1st day Leviticus 23:23-25	7th month, 10th day Leviticus 23:26-32	7th month, 15th day, for 7 days; 8th day, Holy Convocation Leviticus 23:33-44	
	Regathering of Israel in preparation for final day of atonement Jeremiah 32:37-41 	**Israel will repent and look to Messiah in one day** Zechariah 12:10; 13:1; 14:9 	**Families of the earth will come to Jerusalem to celebrate the Feast of Booths** Zechariah 14:16-19 	**New heaven and new earth** **God tabernacles with men** Revelation 21:1-3
	Ezekiel 36:24	Ezekiel 36:25-27 Hebrews 9, 10 Romans 11:25-29	Ezekiel 36:28	

Coming of Christ

Israel had two harvests each year—spring and autumn

Theme of 1 Corinthians:

SEGMENT DIVISIONS

PROBLEMS OR TOPICS	MAJOR SEGMENT DIVISIONS	CHAPTER THEMES
		1
		2
		3
		4
		5
		6
		7
		8
		9
		10
		11
		12
		13
		14
		15
		16

Author:

Date:

Purpose:

Key Words:

Second Corinthians

Introduction

I've always wanted to write a Precept Upon Precept Inductive Study Course on the book of 2 Corinthians and call it, "The Anatomy of a Man of God."

No other New Testament book gives us a clearer and more intimate look at the incredible apostle Paul than 2 Corinthians! In this epistle, Paul bears his soul as he invites us into the rooms of his heart.

As you study this book, once again you will look at God's answers to personal relationships and passions, yet from a different aspect. In 1 Corinthians you saw a fleshly (carnal), divided church beset by problems and full of questions. In 2 Corinthians you will see how a spiritual man of God deals with problematic personal relationships and the passions that are consequently stirred in the deep recesses of his soul as he presses on in the midst of affliction, pain, sorrow, and conflict as a faithful servant of the New Covenant.

This is where you will find your solace if you have determined to be God's man, God's woman in this day and hour—no matter the cost.

WEEK ONE

Why the Sorrow, the Afflictions?

DAY ONE

Of all Paul's epistles, none gives a more intimate glimpse into the life, the heart, and the sufferings of this man than 2 Corinthians. You will not only be blessed, but encouraged and challenged. If you prayerfully study and meditate on its truths, you'll find yourself better prepared for the days ahead, days when your walk and your ministry may be challenged or tested to the very core of its being.

Read through 2 Corinthians 1 and mark in a distinctive way every reference to the author(s) of this epistle. Watch for the personal pronouns that relate to them. If you have completed the 1 Corinthians study you will undoubtedly want to mark the references to Paul in the same way you marked them there. Continue to add your insights to the list you began in the 1 Corinthians study or begin a new list for the insights you'll gain on Paul in 2 Corinthians.

As you read this chapter it will be helpful to consult the map on page 76 so you can see the places Paul refers to in this chapter and others.

Paul's Third Missionary Journey
Acts

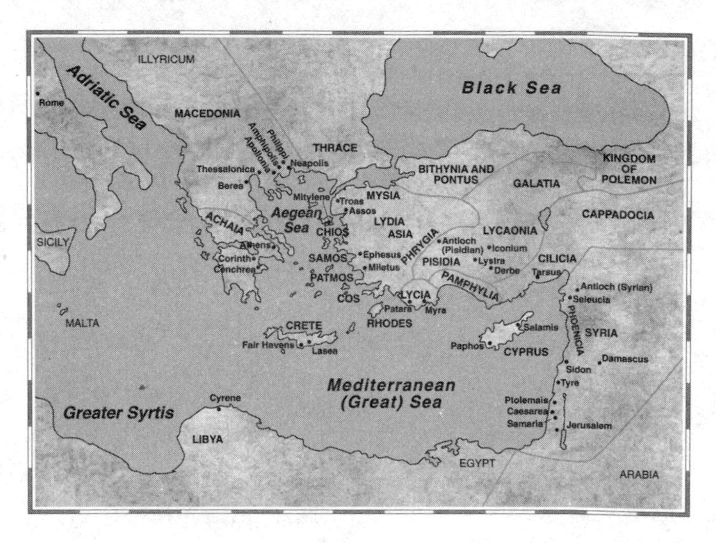

Day Two

Read the first chapter of 2 Corinthians again today, but this time mark every reference to the recipients. When you finish, list in your notebook everything you learn from marking the references to the Corinthians. Again, add to your list from 1 Corinthians or begin a new one.

Day Three

Read through 2 Corinthians 1 again. This time mark each of the following key words in a distinctive way: *comfort*[1] *(comforts,*[2] *comforted*[3]*), affliction*[4] *(afflicted*[5]*)* and *suffer(ings)*. In your notebook make a list of what you learn from marking these three key words.

As you compile your list on the author(s), you will begin to see Paul's purpose in writing. It would also be helpful at this time for you to stop and read 2 Corinthians 12:14–12:3,10, because you will get a preview of why Paul writes as he does and says what he says.

There is a chart, SEQUENCE OF EVENTS IN PAUL'S LIFE AFTER HIS CONVERSION, on page 78 which you will find helpful in seeing what period in Paul's life he wrote 2 Corinthians.

DAY FOUR

Read chapter 2 and once again mark every reference to the author(s), then list what you learn in your notebook.

DAY FIVE

Read 2 Corinthians 1:23–2:17 and mark every reference to the recipients. Also mark the following key words: *sorrow*[6] *(sorrowful)*,[7] *affliction*, *comfort*,[8] *love*, and every reference to Satan, our enemy, and any pronouns that refer to him. As I said previously, I mark every reference to the enemy and to spiritual warfare with a red pitchfork. This makes it easy to spot every reference to Satan.

DAY SIX

Having done all your observations, read through 2 Corinthians 1 and 2 again. As you read look for and mark

Sequence of Events in Paul's Life after His Conversion*

**There are differing opinions on these dates. For continuity's sake this chart will be the basis for dates pertaining to Paul's life.*

Year A.D.	Event
33-34	Conversion, time in Damascus
35-47	Some silent years, except we know that Paul: 1. Spent time in Arabia and Damascus 2. Made first visit to Jerusalem 3. Went to Tarsus, Syria-Cilicia area 4. Was with Barnabas in Antioch 5. With Barnabas took relief to brethren in Judea—Paul's second visit to Jerusalem 6. Returned to Antioch; was sent out with Barnabas by church at Antioch
47-48	First missionary journey: *Galatians written (?)*
49	Apostolic Council at Jerusalem—Paul visits Jerusalem (compare Acts 15 with Galatians 2:1)
49-51	Second missionary journey: *1 and 2 Thessalonians written*
52-56	Third missionary journey: *1 and 2 Corinthians and Romans written*
56	Paul goes to Jerusalem and is arrested; held at Caesarea
57-59	Appearance before Felix and Drusilla; before Festus; before Agrippa
59-60	Appeals to Caesar, sent from Caesarea to Rome
60-62	First Roman imprisonment: *Ephesians, Philemon, Colossians, and Philippians written*
62	Paul's release; possible trip to Spain
62	Paul in Macedonia: *1 Timothy written*
62	Paul goes to Crete: *Titus written*
63-64	Paul taken to Rome and imprisoned: *2 Timothy written*
64	Paul is absent from the body and present with the Lord *(Others put Paul's conversion about A.D. 35, his death in A.D. 68.)*

write[9] *(wrote).* Remember what you observed when you looked at 2 Corinthians 12:14–13:3,10. Paul had been to Corinth twice. He was planning a third visit. Think about the reason for the delay of his visit.

Now look at what you learn from marking *write (wrote).* By noting every reference to the fact that Paul had written to them before, see if you can discern why he wrote then and what that has to do, in part, with his reason for writing now.

Record the main themes of chapters 1 and 2 on the 2 CORINTHIANS AT A GLANCE chart at the end of this study.

DAY SEVEN

Store in your heart: 2 Corinthians 1:3,4.

Read and discuss: 2 Corinthians 1:1-11; 2:1-11 (Do this one passage at a time.)

OPTIONAL QUESTIONS FOR DISCUSSION

- What did you learn from 2 Corinthians 1 about sufferings and afflictions? Examine what the text teaches you in the light of the 5 W's and an H.
- Why do you think Paul brings up the subject of afflictions and comfort from the very beginning of his letter?
  a. Where was Paul when he was burdened excessively?

b. How severe were his afflictions?

c. Was he alone when he suffered these afflictions?

d. According to Paul, what was the source of help at this time?

- From what you studied this week, what can you discern about Paul's reason for writing this epistle to the Corinthians?

- According to the 2 Corinthians 2:1-11 passage, why had Paul written them previously?

- According to 2 Corinthians 2:6-11 what apparently happened and what were they to do about it now? Why? Be specific in your answer, giving the verses or portion of the verses that support your answer.

  a. What do you learn regarding the enemy, Satan, in this passage?

  b. How important is forgiveness? Why?

- Second Corinthians is an epistle that gives you insight into the anatomy of a man of God. Therefore, glean everything you can about Paul from this epistle. What did you learn from marking all the references to Paul (and Timothy) in these first two chapters?

Thought for the Week

What kind of a fragrance does your life exude? Does the way you live, the way you respond to afflictions and sufferings, the way you relate to people manifest the sweet aroma of the knowledge of Christ?

Do you "peddle" or "corrupt" the Word of God? Do you corrupt it by your life, your appetites, your relationships, or do people sense the sincerity of your commitment to Him?

Please realize that even though you may be a sweet aroma of Him, to some you will be more like an aroma of death. Your life will stand in such direct opposition to

the lives of the ungodly that they will hate you because of your righteousness and your confession and proclamation of the glorious gospel of Christ.

But do not despair, whether you are a fragrance of life unto life to those who will believe, or death unto death to those who will not and who desire to get rid of you, you are a sweet fragrance of Christ to God.

In all your sufferings and afflictions He is there to comfort you. Just remember, where there is abundant suffering there is also abundant comfort. That comfort is not just for you, but for others as well. When you are comforted by God, you know how to comfort others.

May your proud confidence be that in holiness and godly sincerity, in the grace of God, you conduct yourself in a way that demonstrates the reality of your relationship with Jesus Christ.

WEEK TWO

What Is Your Relationship to the New Covenant? What Has It Cost You?

DAY ONE

To get a better perspective on why this book was written, simply read chapters 1–7 in 2 Corinthians. If you see any reference to the reason for writing, underline or mark it in a distinctive way.

DAY TWO

Reading chapters 10–13 will give you insight into Paul's relationship with the Corinthians as well as a clearer understanding of the purpose of his writing. You will also gain an overview of the book as you read these three chapters. Once again, if you see any reference to the reasons for writing, underline or mark them in a distinctive way.

DAY THREE

Read 2 Corinthians 3. Mark every reference to the author(s) and to the recipients. Also mark *adequate*[10] or *adequacy*.[11] Then go back and mark *adequate*[12] in 2:16. In your notebook record what you learn about the author, the recipients, and about adequacy.

DAY FOUR

Now read through chapter 3 again. Mark every reference to the *Spirit*[13] along with any pronouns and every occurrence of the word *veil*[14] *(unveiled).*[15] Then go back to 1:22 and mark the word *Spirit* there also.

Note the two ministries mentioned in this chapter and how they are referred to or described, i.e., what terms or synonyms are used to describe them? In a distinctive color (or way), mark the references to these two ministries so you can tell one from the other. Don't forget to mark any pronouns referring to them. Then list in your notebook what this chapter teaches regarding each of these ministries[16] or covenants.[17]

DAY FIVE

Read 2 Corinthians 4. Mark the following words: *veiled, afflicted*[18] *(affliction*[19]*)* (mark these words as you marked *affliction* and *afflicted* in chapters 1 and 2), *gospel, death (dying), life (live).*[20] Also mark the word *ministry* in accordance with which ministry it is and how you marked it in chapter 3.

DAY SIX

Read through 2 Corinthians 3 and 4 again. This time

mark every reference to *Jesus Christ* (*Jesus, Lord, Christ*). Be sure to include any pronouns. Make a list in your notebook of all you learn about Him from these two chapters. (Did you mark the reference to Satan as *the god of this world*[21]?)

Finally, don't forget to record the themes of chapters 3 and 4 on the AT A GLANCE chart.

DAY SEVEN

Store in your heart: 2 Corinthians 4:16-18.
Read and discuss: 2 Corinthians 3:1–4; 4:15–18.

OPTIONAL QUESTIONS FOR DISCUSSION

- From your survey reading of 2 Corinthians this week, and from 2 Corinthians 3:1 specifically, what do you sense is taking place between Paul and the Corinthian Christians? What Scriptures can you use to support your view?
- What two covenants[22] (ministries) are set forth in 2 Corinthians 3 and how are they described?
- What was Moses' purpose in veiling his face when he came down from Sinai after receiving the Law?
  a. What do you learn about the Old Covenant from this passage?
  b. What was Paul's ministry that he refers to in 4:1?
  c. What do you learn from these chapters about those who do not receive or believe in Jesus Christ?

- Twice in 2 Corinthians 4, Paul says that they do not lose heart (do not faint). What could cause them to lose heart? What would keep them from losing heart?
- What did you learn from marking the contrasting words *death* and *life* in 2 Corinthians 4? How can you apply what you learned to your own life?
- What do you learn about afflictions (troubles) from 2 Corinthians 4?
- What do you learn about the Lord Jesus Christ by marking every reference to Him in these two chapters?

THOUGHT FOR THE WEEK

What an awesome calling you have as child of God—the privilege of being a servant of the New Covenant! The covenant you minister is not one of death and condemnation, but one of life, righteousness, and the Spirit.

The Old Covenant could only show a man his sin and try to hold him in line — but the New Covenant is another matter!

The New Covenant not only gives life, but it also provides the Spirit of God. And from the Spirit of God comes our adequacy:

- the Spirit brings liberty,
- the Spirit transforms us into the image of our beloved Lord, as we behold His glory,
- the Spirit indwells these common earthen vessels,
- the Spirit brings us into situations of death where the

life of Christ might be manifested so clearly that others might see and desire Jesus also,

- the Spirit sustains us in these momentary light afflictions and, thus, produces an eternal weight of glory far beyond all comparison, and
- the Spirit enables us to look beyond the temporal to the eternal.

O Father, thank You for this ministry! May we stamp eternity upon our eyes.

Week Three

What Controls You in How You Live and How You Relate to Others?

Day One

What are the unseen things you must keep before you? Things that you must know, that you must remember? Read 2 Corinthians 5, then write out the question and your insights in your notebook.

Day Two

Read 2 Corinthians 5:1-10 and observe that Paul refers to two different dwellings. Mark each dwelling in a distinctive way. Then, in your notebook, record what these dwellings are, what takes place in them, and how it all comes about.

Mark the word *Spirit* and note what role the Spirit plays in all this.

Day Three

Read chapter 5 again today and mark every reference to the author(s). Also mark every occurrence of the word *reconciled (reconciling, reconciliation).*

Read the chapter again and mark every reference to the Corinthians. List all you learn about the author(s) and the recipients in your notebook.

DAY FOUR

Again read chapter 5 marking every reference to Jesus Christ. Then, in your notebook, list what you learn from marking these references to Him. When you finish, meditate on what you observed and then talk to God about the things you noticed.

DAY FIVE

Read through chapters 6 and 7 and mark every reference to the author(s) and every reference to the recipients. If, when Paul uses the pronouns "*we*" or "*us*" you believe he refers to both the authors and the recipients, combine the colors you are using for each in marking that reference. Then you can see how the authors are relating to the recipients or how they are including them in whatever they are saying.

Now read through chapters 6 and 7 one more time. As you do, mark the following key words: *comfort*[23] *(comforts,*[24] *comforted*[25]*)*, and *affliction(s)*[26] *(afflicted*[27]*)*. Also mark the words *sorrow*[28] and *sorrowful*[29] and notice the contrast between the two kinds of sorrow. As you did before, mark *wrote* (mark *letter*[30] in the same way you mark *wrote* since that was what Paul wrote).

DAY SIX

List all you learned about the author(s) and about the recipients in your notebook. You will discover more about Paul's relationship with the Corinthians and possibly gain insight into part of the source of the problems in Corinth.

Record the themes of chapters 5, 6, and 7 on the 2 CORINTHIANS AT A GLANCE chart.

DAY SEVEN

Store in your heart: 2 Corinthians 5:8-10 and 2 Corinthians 5:21.

Read and discuss: 2 Corinthians 5; Romans 14:7-12.

OPTIONAL QUESTIONS FOR DISCUSSION

- What did you learn from chapter 5 about death and what happens when a believer dies?
  - a. What effect did these realities have on Paul and Timothy?
  - b. What did they know awaited them after death?
  - c. How important are a Christian's deeds?
- Discuss what 2 Corinthians 5:10 and Romans 14:7-12 teach in respect to the judgment seat of Christ. Examine these verses by asking the 5 W's and an H.
- According to 2 Corinthians 5 what controlled Paul?

a. What had Paul concluded and how did this affect his relationship with those who now belonged to Christ?

b. What do you think Paul means when he says, "from now on we recognize no man according to the flesh"?[31]

- What was Paul and Timothy's ministry? Explain what you learned from marking every reference to reconciliation.
- What are the various ways Paul and Timothy commended themselves as servants of Christ? As you look at the commendations in 2 Corinthians 6:1-10, look at what Paul calls them in 4:17.
- From all you studied this week, why do you think the Corinthians were restrained in their affection towards Paul and Timothy?
- What were some of the things and emotions Paul and Timothy had to deal with? According to them, how did they make it?
- What two kinds of sorrow are mentioned in chapter 7? What is the end of each?
- How do Paul and Timothy encourage the Corinthians, despite the conflicts they experienced within the Corinthian church?
- What can you learn from this example to help you with your relationships, especially with those who might be critical of you for various reasons?

THOUGHT FOR THE WEEK

Paul's Christianity was not mere theology. He wholeheartedly embraced truth. He studied it, knew it, and lived accordingly. Eternity was stamped upon his eyes; he was well aware of life after death—therefore the fear of death never held him in its grip. Yes, Paul tells us in the opening chapter of this epistle that they despaired of life, that the sentence of death was within them. But even then Paul saw an opportunity from God—not to trust in himself, but in God. Paul was absolutely convinced that the minute he was absent from his body he would be with the Lord, that mortality would be swallowed up in immortality. Thus Paul's driving passion was to be pleasing to God, whether at "home" in his body or present with the Lord.

Paul also knew that one day he, along with every other believer, would stand at the judgment seat of Christ. Just as there was a *bēma* seat (judgment seat) in Corinth, so there was one in heaven, and Paul "feared" the Lord enough to live accordingly. He lived for God, not for man, nor for self. Paul knew the forgiveness of God and the love of Christ, and that knowledge embraced and controlled him. It constrained him to one purpose: the ministry of reconciliation.

This purpose was one of the reasons Paul would not write off the Corinthians. He would not discount "the good" in them because of that which was bad, that which hurt him. He would keep them in his heart whether or not they opened their hearts wide to him. He had begotten them in Christ and he would not forsake them, even if many criticized him and cast doubts on the authenticity of his ministry. In all that Paul had suffered, he had commended himself as a servant of Christ, so he would not stop now. He would be what he was supposed to be. He would not stop being honest with them. He would deal with sin—even if it caused them sorrow. He would not forsake his God-given responsibility toward them. They, too, would stand at the judgment seat, and he did not want them to be ashamed.

Therefore, Paul held his ground, even against the unbelievers who came in among the Corinthians to turn them away from him and from his God-ordained authority and leadership. Paul would not give up. Whatever was needed, Paul would do it. But he would always do it within the confines of the truth he believed and lived.

O Beloved, when it comes to difficult relationships, may you follow Paul's example no matter the personal cost! May you live what you believe and may you remember there is only One whom you need to please at all times—and that is our Lord.

WEEK FOUR

How Much Do You Care? How Far Does Your Devotion Go?

DAY ONE

Read 2 Corinthians 8 and 9. As you read, mark the following words: *grace* or *gracious work*.[32] Watch for any synonymous terms that would refer to the "grace of God which has been given in the churches of Macedonia" (2 Corinthians 8:1), that is, the gracious work that Paul wants the Corinthians to also carry out. Mark these synonymous terms in the same way you marked *grace* and *gracious work*.

When you finish reading this chapter, stop and think about what happens to the Corinthians at this point. In your notebook record what grace, what gracious work, Paul is referring to.

DAY TWO

Read through 2 Corinthians 8 and 9 again. Make a chart with three columns in your notebook using these headings: THE MACEDONIANS, CHRIST, and THE CORINTHIANS. Now record on the chart what you learn about the churches in Macedonia. (Paul was in

Macedonia when he wrote 2 Corinthians.) Next, list what you learn about Christ's example as put forth in these chapters. Tomorrow we will look at the Corinthians.

DAY THREE

Read through chapters 8 and 9 and mark every reference to the Corinthians. Then, on the chart you began yesterday, record what you learn about the Corinthians in respect to this ministry to the saints—the ministry of giving.

DAY FOUR

One final day on 2 Corinthians 8 and 9! Read through these chapters again, and in your notebook make a list of all the principles related to the ministry of giving. You will find this list profitable, enlightening, and practical. When you finish your list, ask God to show you how to live in accordance with what these chapters teach.

If you have time, you might want to look up some other New Testament passages and think about what they teach about those who labor in the gospel: Galatians 6:6-10; 1 Corinthians 9:3-11; 1 Thessalonians 5:12,13; Ephesians 4:28; and 1 Timothy 5:8; 6:17-19. As you read, list what you learn in your notebook.

DAY FIVE

Read through 2 Corinthians 10 and mark every reference to the author(s). Notice what subject Paul has returned to. What further insight can you glean from this chapter regarding Paul's situation with the Corinthian church?

DAY SIX

Read through chapter 10 and mark every reference to the Corinthians. List what you learn in your notebook.

Paul uses the words *commend(s),*[33] *commendation,*[34] and *commending*[35] throughout 2 Corinthians. He also uses the words *boast,*[36] *boasts,*[37] *boasted,* and *boasting.*[38] Look up each of the references listed below and mark the two words (with their forms) in a distinctive way, if you have not already marked them in your Bible. Cover only the first ten chapters. Next week we will see how boast is used again.

commend 3:1; 10:12
commends 10:18
commending 4:2; 5:12; 6:4
commendation 3:1
boast 9:2; 10:8,13,16,17
boasts 10:17
boasted 7:14
boasting 7:4,14; 8:24; 9:3; 10:15

(Remember, if you are using the NIV, KJV, or NKJV, check the equivalents cited in the previous footnotes.)

When you finish, analyze what you learn from marking these words. Record your insights in your notebook.

Don't forget to record the chapter themes on the 2 CORINTHIANS AT A GLANCE chart.

DAY SEVEN

Store in your heart: 2 Corinthians 10:3,4 or preferably 10:3-5.

Read and discuss: 2 Corinthians 10:1-12.

OPTIONAL QUESTIONS FOR DISCUSSION

- What subject does Paul return to after 2 Corinthians 8 and 9?
  - a. What does this tell you about the gravity of this subject as it relates to Paul?
  - b. What was the theme of 2 Corinthians 8 and 9?
  - c. Does Paul mention this subject again in chapter 10? How? (Look at 2 Corinthians 10:13-16.)
- From reading chapter 10, how do you think Paul sees this conflict with the Corinthians? What kind of battle is it?
- According to 2 Corinthians 10:3-6 what is a person to do in this kind of a warfare?
- From this chapter, how would you define a strong hold or fortress?
- Do you think people have strongholds or fortresses of wrong thinking or belief today? What might some of these be? What form might they take?

- What form did they take in Paul's case?
  a. What was being said about Paul that he could either believe or submit to God and to His Word? Which did Paul choose to do?
  b. What was the result of his choice?
  c. What do you think would have occurred in Paul or in his ministry if he had listened to, embraced, or believed the lies of the enemy? Remember, his warfare was with the enemy rather than flesh and blood.
- If there is time, look up the following verses and note what you learn about the enemy and some of his tactics:
  a. John 8:44
  b. Revelation 12:10,11
  c. Ephesians 6:11,12
  d. 2 Corinthians 2:10,11
  e. Ephesians 4:25-27 (The word *opportunity*[39] literally means "a place of occupation."[40])

THOUGHT FOR THE WEEK

It seems from 2 Corinthians 10:4,5 that a stronghold or fortress is a speculation (rather than a fact) or a belief or thought that is contrary to the knowledge of God. It is contrary to what God is, what He says, and what He commands, but it is what a person chooses to believe, dwell on, embrace, and thus be controlled by. A stronghold or fortress would be like a command post of the devil, for he is a liar and the father of lies. He did not and does not abide in the truth. As a matter of fact, according to Genesis 3:1, the first recorded words of the devil, the serpent of old, Satan, were "Yea, hath God said . . ." (KJV).

The enemy gains a stronghold when he gets us to think contrary to the Word of God. That's why the enemy's primary goal is to keep us from the Word of God—from knowing truth, from knowing we are loved unconditionally by Him, from knowing that we were chosen in Christ Jesus before the foundation of the world. The enemy doesn't want us to realize that we are precious in His sight, that there is no condemnation now that we are in Christ, that we are new creatures in Christ and that old things have passed away, that all things in our lives will work together for good.

Are there any strongholds (fortresses) that you need to destroy? What are they? Are you going to allow the enemy to hold the fort in your thinking or are you going to take the weapons of warfare and use them on him? Remember, "Greater is He [Christ] who is in you than he who is in the world" (1 John 4:4). The prince of this world has only a short time left . . . Christ will reign forever. Let Christ begin to reign now over every aspect of your thinking, of your being. Believe God.

This, Beloved, is why Jesus prayed, "Father . . . I do not ask Thee to take them out of the world, but to keep them from the evil one. They are not of the world, even as I am not of the world. Sanctify them in the truth; Thy word is truth" (John 17:1,15-17).

Unbelief . . . sin begins in the mind. So, Satan targets your mind. Satan had targeted the minds of some of the people in Corinth and the church was in danger of listening to them, of believing them. Satan would have loved nothing better; if he could separate them from Paul, from his authority, from his teaching, from his love, then Satan could sift them as wheat.

Satan is into destroying relationships, and he is having a heyday simply because we are not doing what Paul did. We are not bringing every thought captive to the obedience of Christ and we are not being quick to punish all disobedience. Paul, even if he had to boast, would not back down to the enemy's lies. He continued to love, continued to pursue, and continued to stand for truth.

O Beloved, where are you in all this? There is a battle raging for the minds of men, for as a man thinks, so he is. Saturate yourself with the Word of God and believe and live accordingly. Yes, it is warfare, but God will always lead you in triumph if you will allow Him to lead!

WEEK FIVE

What Will You Boast In—Your Experiences or Your Weaknesses?

DAY ONE

Read 2 Corinthians 11. As you did last week, mark every reference to *boast* or *boasting*.[41] Also mark every reference to Satan (along with all the appropriate pronouns and synonyms) in a distinctive way. In the same way you mark Satan, mark every reference to spirits that are connected with him. You might also want to go back to chapter 10 and mark the reference to *warfare*[42] in the same way. When you finish, add to your list on boasting in your notebook.

DAY TWO

Today read through 2 Corinthians 11 again. Mark every reference to the author(s) and to the recipients. List in your notebook what you learn about each from this chapter.

When you finish, think about what Paul and Timothy are saying in this chapter. Do you sense an increased intensity? What do you see Paul doing in this chapter? Does it point out to you how serious Paul is about what is happening in Corinth with respect to him and his role and relationship with the church there?

Think about what you learn about this man of God, and what even a godly leader can go through. Feel for Paul. Learn from Paul. Persevere like Paul.

DAY THREE

Read 2 Corinthians 11:30–12:21. Mark every occurrence of the word *boast*[43] or *boasting* as you have done previously. Also mark every reference to Paul.

Note the irony Paul uses in his writing in this chapter. It will give you insight into what people were accusing him of.

DAY FOUR

Read chapter 12 again. Mark the word *grace* and note its connection to power (strength). Also mark any reference to Satan.

When you finish reading and marking this chapter, think about what is recorded in the first ten verses of this chapter. Examine this experience in light of the 5 W's and an H.

DAY FIVE

Read through chapter 12 again and this time mark

every reference to the recipients of this letter. Then list everything you learn about Paul and the recipients.

At this point in your study, it would be helpful to look at every reference to Satan that you have marked in 2 Corinthians and make a list in your notebook of all you learn from these references. When you finish, think about how these insights can help you.

DAY SIX

Read 2 Corinthians 13 and mark every reference to the recipients and to the author(s). Mark any key words that you have marked previously in this epistle.

Watch how Paul compares the "weakness" he is accused of with the Lord's weakness.

What do you sense as Paul brings this epistle to a close? How does the way he closes compare with the way he began?

For the final time, list what you learn about the author(s) and the recipients in your notebook. When you have time, you would find it quite beneficial to review this list and meditate—especially on all that this epistle tells you about Paul. Truly this is the anatomy of a man of God—someone you and I can imitate.

Don't forget to record your themes for chapters 11, 12, and 13 on your AT A GLANCE chart.

DAY SEVEN

Store in your heart: 2 Corinthians 12:9,10.
Read and discuss: 2 Corinthians 11:1-4,12-15; 12:1-10.

OPTIONAL QUESTIONS FOR DISCUSSION

- According to 2 Corinthians 11:1-4, what were Paul's concerns for the church at Corinth?
  - a. Why was Paul jealous for them?
  - b. Do you see any parallel between 2 Corinthians 11:2 and 1 Corinthians 4:14,15?
  - c. How susceptible were the Corinthians to Satan? Do you think Paul's description of them in 1 Corinthians 3:1-4 and 1 Corinthians 1:11,12 reflects why they were so susceptible?
- What do you learn about the enemy from 2 Corinthians 11:12-15?
- Describe Paul's experience as related in 2 Corinthians 11:23–12:10.
  - a. What do you learn about Paradise and the third heaven from this passage?
  - b. How does Paul treat this experience?
  - c. Did Paul exploit this experience? Does this give you a possible pattern or example in respect to those today who claim to have had similar experiences?
  - d. What do you learn about "a messenger of Satan" from this passage?
  - e. What do you learn about grace from this passage? How sufficient, how powerful is grace?
  - f. How could Paul be strong when he was weak?
  - g. What can you learn from all this about your own life?

- As Paul brought his epistle to a close, did you notice any change in the way he dealt with the Corinthian church? Why do you suppose this was?
- What did you learn from making your list about the Corinthians? How did God speak to your heart, either to warn, admonish, correct, or encourage you?
- What do you think Paul is saying in 2 Corinthians 13:5? Do you think it is good for people who claim to know Christ to examine themselves? Give your reasons, then examine whether or not your reasons are biblical or simply emotional or according to your own reasoning.
- What did you learn from this letter about our responsibility to one another as Christians? or as an older Christian to a younger? or as a spiritual parent to a child in the gospel?
- What did you learn from Paul and from Timothy about what it is like to serve the Lord fully? What spoke to you the most as you made all your lists about these men and their experiences?
- As you bring this study to a close, think about how these truths can or will affect the way you live. It would be good to close in prayer for one another.

THOUGHT FOR THE WEEK

Someday, Beloved, you are going to see your heavenly Bridegroom face-to-face. What kind of a bride will you be on that day? Will you be one who has kept herself pure, one who has prepared a beautiful gown through righteousnesses as Revelation 19:7-9 says?

That day is coming sooner than you think—your days on earth are merely a vapor in comparison to eternity with the Lord Jesus Christ. You and I are living in the last days, the consummation of the ages.

When this earthly tent is torn down, when you receive your eternal home from heaven, when you look into the eyes of your Bridegroom, will He see a bride who has lived in purity and devotion to Him? When the rewards are given at the judgment seat of Christ what will you receive?

When you see Him face-to-face, will others be there with you—others you can boast in with godly boasting because you introduced them to Christ, birthed them, and cared for them as a parent should care for his child?

Have you provided them with an example they can follow—the example of being and remaining a servant of God no matter the hardships, the difficulties, the weaknesses? Have you demonstrated to them the sufficiency and power of His grace which is perfected in your weakness?

If so, Beloved, you will hear "Well done, good and faithful slave . . . enter into the joy of your master" (Matthew 25:21). And joy it will be—an eternal weight of glory beyond all comparison!

Since you have the ministry of the New Covenant and you have received mercy, don't lose heart; rather, say with Paul, "but we have renounced the things hidden because of shame, not walking in craftiness or adulterating the word of God, but by the manifestation of truth commending ourselves to every man's conscience in the sight of God" (2 Corinthians 4:2).

Theme of 2 Corinthians:

SEGMENT DIVISIONS

		CHAPTER THEMES
		1
		2
		3
		4
		5
		6
		7
		8
		9
		10
		11
		12
		13

Author:

Date:

Purpose:

Key Words:

comfort (comforted)

afflicted (affliction, suffer, sufferings)

sorrow(ful)

boast (boasting or glory, as both are from the same Greek root word)

confidence

commend(ing)

death

life

heart

joy (rejoice, rejoicing, rejoiced)

ministry

grace

Titus

mark references to the enemy (warfare, serpent, Satan, as well as relative pronouns and synonyms)

NOTES

FIRST CORINTHIANS

1. NKJV; KJV: *schism*
2. KJV; NKJV: also *strength*
3. NASB: Also mark the word *cleverness* in 1:17. According to the reference note, *cleverness* literally means *wisdom*; NIV: *expert, sensible*
4. KJV: *glory (glorieth, glorying);* NKJV: also *glory (glories, glorying)*
5. NIV: *now for, now about*
   KJV: also *now as*
6. NIV: "Now for the matters you wrote about"
   KJV: "Now concerning the things whereof ye wrote unto me"
   NKJV: "Now concerning the things of which you wrote to me"
7. NIV: "Now about food sacrificed to idols"
   KJV: "Now as touching things offered unto idols"
   NKJV: "Now concerning things offered to idols"
8. KJV: Mark *Holy Ghost* and *Spirit* when it refers to the Holy Spirit
9. KJV: *husbandry*
10. KJV; NKJV: *glory*
11. NIV: also *sexually immoral, sins sexually*
    NKJV: also *fornicator, sexual immorality*
12. NIV; NKJV: *sexual immorality*
    KJV; NKJV: *fornicator(s), fornication*
13. NKJV: also *judgments*
14. NIV: also *sexually immoral, sins sexually*
    NKJV: also *sexual immorality, fornicator*
15. NIV; NKJV: *sexually immoral*
    KJV: *fornicator(s), fornication(s)*
16. NIV: Does not use *marriage.*
17. NIV: *immorality*
    KJV: *fornication*
    NKJV: *sexual immorality*
18. NIV: *not a believer*
    KJV: *believeth not*
    NKJV: *does not believe*

19. NIV: also *not a believer, unbeliever*
    KJV: also *believeth not*
    NKJV: also *does not believe*
20. NKJV: also *calling*
21. KJV: *carefulness, careth*
    NKJV: *care(s)*
21. NIV: *unmarried, divorce*
    KJV; NKJV: *loosed*
23. KJV: *glorying, glory*
    NKJV: *boasting*
24. NIV; KJV: also use *law*
25. KJV; NKJV: *Moreover*
26. NIV: *forefathers*
27. KJV: also *ensamples*
28. NASB: In 10:10 also mark *did* as it also refers to *grumbled.*
    KJV; NKJV: *murmur, murmured*
29. KJV: *devils*
30. NIV: also *recognizing*
    KJV: also *damnation, discerning, condemnation*
    NKJV: also *discerning*
31. KJV; NKJV: *schism*
32. KJV; NKJV: *schism*
33. KJV: *Holy Ghost*
34. NIV: *part(s)*
35. NIV; KJV; NKJV: also *prophecies*
36. KJV: *charity*
37. NIV: also *strengthening*
38. NIV: *different kinds*
    KJV; NKJV: *diversities, differences*
39. NIV: *passed on*
40. KJV: *grave, slept*
41. KJV: *rose, rise(n)*
    NKJV: also uses *rose, rise(n)*
42. KJV: also *charity*
43. NIV: *be men of courage*
    KJV: *quit you like men*
    NKJV: *be brave*

SECOND CORINTHIANS

1. KJV; NKJV: also *consolation*
2. KJV: *comforteth*
3. KJV: *consolation*
4. NIV: *troubles, afflictions*
   KJV; NKJV: *tribulation, trouble*
5. NIV: *distressed*
6. NIV: also *painful, grieve(d), distressed, grief*
   KJV: also *heaviness, sorry, grief, grieved*
   NKJV: also *grief*
7. NIV: *grieve(d)*
   NKJV: also *grieved*
8. KJV: also *consolation*
9. NKJV: *writing*
10. KJV: *sufficient, able*
    NKJV: *sufficient*
11. NIV: *competent*
    KJV; NKJV: *sufficiency*
12. NIV: *equal*
    KJV; NKJV: *sufficient*
13. NKJV: Only mark *Spirit (spirit)* when it refers to the Holy Spirit.
14. KJV: *vail*
15. KJV: also *open*
16. KJV: ministration
17. KJV: testament
    NKJV: Testament
18. NIV; NKJV: *hard pressed*
    KJV: *troubled*
19. NIV: *troubles*
20. NIV: *are alive*
21. NIV; NKJV: *the god of this age*
22. KJV: testaments
23. NIV: also *encouraged, encouragement*
    KJV; NKJV: also *consolation*
24. KJV: *comforteth*
25. NIV: also *encouraged*
26. NIV: *troubles*
    KJV; NKJV: *tribulation(s)*

27. NIV: *harassed*
    KJV; NKJV: *troubled*
28. KJV: also *sorry, sorrowed*
29. NIV; KJV; NKJV: *sorry*
30. KJV; NKJV: also *epistle*
31. NIV: "from now on we regard no one from a worldly point of view"
    KJV: "henceforth know we no man after the flesh"
    NKJV: "from now on, we regard no one according to the flesh"
32. NIV: *act of grace*, also *grace of giving, offering*
    KJV; NKJV: *gracious work* not used, so only mark *grace* in the KJV and *grace* and *gift* in the NKJV.
33. KJV: also *commendeth*
34. NIV: *recommendation*
35. KJV: also *approving*
36. KJV; NKJV: also *glory*
37. KJV: *glorieth*
    NKJV: *glories*
38. NIV: also *pride*
    KJV: also *glorying*
39. NIV: *foothold*
    KJV; NKJV: *place*
40. Spiros Zodhiates defines opportunity as "to make room."
41. KJV: also *glory*
42. NIV: *fight with*
43. KJV: also *glory*

Books in the International Inductive Study Series

Teach Me Your Ways
Genesis, Exodus, Leviticus, Numbers, Deuteronomy

The Call to Follow Jesus
Luke

The Holy Spirit Unleashed in You
Acts

Free from Bondage God's Way
Galatians, Ephesians

God's Answers for Relationships and Passions
1 & 2 Corinthians

Choosing Victory, Overcoming Defeat
Joshua, Judges, Ruth

Also by Kay Arthur

How to Study Your Bible

Beloved

His Imprint, My Expression

God, Are You There?

Lord, Teach Me to Pray in 28 Days

With an Everlasting Love

YES! I am interested in information that will direct me to an inductive Bible-study group in my area *or* that will help me become involved in inductive Bible study on my own.

Please have Precept Ministries contact me with details that will help me begin my inductive study right away!

NAME: ______________________________

ADDRESS: ______________________________

CITY: ______________ STATE: ________ ZIP: __________

TELEPHONE NUMBER: (   ) ______________________

Precept Ministries exists for the sole purpose of establishing God's people in His Word. The ministry serves hundreds of thousands of people across North America and around the globe by offering multiple and varied opportunities for inductive Bible study.

No Postage Necessary If Mailed in the United States

YOUR STAMP WILL HELP THE MINISTRY SAVE MONEY

BUSINESS REPLY MAIL

First Class Mail Permit No. 48 Chattanooga TN

POSTAGE WILL BE PAID BY ADDRESSEE

Precept Ministries
P.O. Box 182218
Chattanooga TN 37422-9901